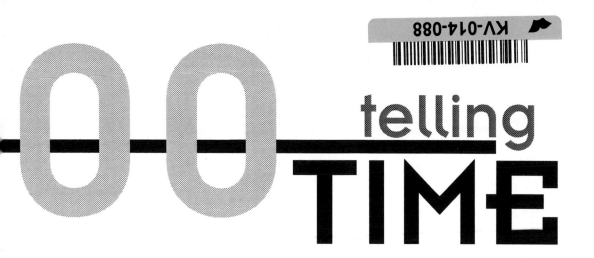

telling TIME

Papers, performances and images from Playworks' *Playing With Time* Festival
held at the Wharf Theatre, Sydney 13-15 October 1995

Australia Council
for the Arts

NSW Government Ministry
For The Arts

Edited by Virginia Baxter and Caitlin Newton-Broad
Photographic collages by Heidrun Löhr

Playworks is assisted by the Australia Council,
the federal government's arts advisory body, and by the NSW Ministry for the Arts.

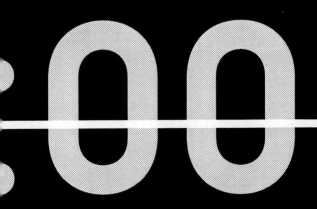

contents

contents

preface

A true festival—
exuberant, celebratory and with
a great spirit of collective affirmation.
Playworks is a genuine pioneering women's organisation.
Pioneering in the 1990's? Sure.
This emerged in discussions with
some of the long term campaigners
like Dorothy Hewett and Katharine Brisbane
but also in the cross-cultural initiatives being taken by
Noëlle Janaczewska, Andrea Aloise, Tes Lyssiotis.
Retrospectives among explorers
are always much more interesting
than they are amongst celebrities:
how did we get here — and where to next?
The questions are still leading the way.

Jane Goodall, University of Western Sydney

This book documents the event, *Playing With Time* — a festival celebrating Playworks' tenth birthday and a decade of Australian women's writing for theatre and performance was held at Sydney Theatre Company, Wharf II, on the weekend of 13-15 October, 1995.

To coincide with the Festival, Playworks conducted a survey on the experiences of some 90 women writers across Australia, and employed researchers in each state to document the programming histories of theatre companies in relation to women's writing. The findings were both exhilarating and alarming. Certainly there is a sense of energy among women writing for performance — a sense that they have gained in skill and experience, that much work is flourishing and more is on the way. However, despite affirmative action policies of governments and the work of development agencies such as Playworks there has been little significant change in the proportion of plays by women produced by mainstage theatre companies across Australia. The need for affirmative action has *definitely* not passed. Material from our questionnaires and state researchers was edited by Colleen Chesterman and published in *Playing With Time: Women Writers for Performance*. The Festival opened on Friday night with the launch of this publication by Caroline Block (Director-General NSW Department for Women) and Sarah Gardiner (Strategy & Communications Branch, Australia Council), whose departments jointly funded the survey.

As part of the celebrations, Playworks invited leading English performance writer Deborah Levy to Australia to conduct workshops in Melbourne, Sydney and Brisbane. We had met Deborah at the International Women Playwrights' Conference in Adelaide in 1994 and saw strong connections between her ideas on identity and performance and the work of Australian women writers across many areas of contemporary performance. A special grant from the Performing Arts Board of the Australia Council allowed us to invite Deborah back to Australia to work with a group of these artists on a version of her *The B-File*—an erotic interrogation of female personae, all with the name Beatrice. This presentation opened the festival. While she was in Australia, Deborah also conducted workshops in Melbourne and Brisbane and collaborated with Suzanne Chaundy on a production of her work at La Mama.

The Event

Scenario: Everything is quiet except for the surreal clock face table on the stage. Oddly, the director's desk is still set up amidst the audience's seats. The table is ticking. Video screens wait, staring. Time for something to happen.

The format for the *Playing With Time* festival was a series of personal diaries of the decade from a range of Australian women writers for theatre and performance. We decided against the conventional conference set-up. Instead, on stage, a large clock face table melted into the floor, the numbers flying across the stage. At the back, two large projection screens and two video monitors for the live video cameras captured the events of the weekend in closeup. A small desk with light was set up in the midst of the audience— as though the production was still 'in rehearsal'. Each of the writers was asked to speak for twenty minutes and to prepare to be interrupted. For each session, a timekeeper performed a simple action marking the passing of the time.

The interrupted diary format was designed to break with the more familiar 'podiums and panels' conference, to create a more performative event which would challenge writers, commentators and audience. We were thrilled with the way writers responded so inventively to the idea of their own diary of the decade and the way the commentators came up with all sorts of creative 'interruptions'.

In asking writers to describe their writing histories we hoped to counter the idea that writers' careers follow one 'onwards and upwards' trajectory. By refusing to put writers on panels and ask them to speak about 'eroticism' or 'the politics of funding' we hoped to encourage a free discussion of aesthetic and cultural questions focussing on writing itself and its production for performance.

Noëlle Janaczewska, Playworks Committee

The space became theatrical with Michelle Dado's wonderful Dali-esque clockface table. Live video cameras operated by Luci Dayhew and Bonnie Elliot, two young film-makers from University of Technology Sydney, caught the interruptions on large monitors. Chairs were replaced by Timekeepers who kept an eye on the sessions while actively passing the 'real' time (reading, counting money, paring apples and pairing socks, peeling artichokes, taking notes, turning the pages of a book).

Throughout the weekend, a number of writer-performers like Nikki Heywood, Andrea Aloise, Deborah Pollard and Victoria Spence "interrupted" proceedings with short performances. The work of such writers is mostly produced outside mainstage venues and is often inappropriately categorised as "non-text based" or "physically-based" and therefore somehow "not writing". However, many do use language in very inventive ways and those who don't, still write highly structured scenarios for performance, eg. Amanda Stewart's writing is for live sound art performances for radio or live performance with musicians. Playworks has an expansive approach to writing and performance; acknowledging that these new forms offer freedoms outside the structures of playwriting and are attracting more and more women writers.

I am amazed that the antagonism which so often pervades relations between those working in 'legit' theatre and other presumably illegitimate and promiscuous performance practices, seems absent here.

Sarah Miller, Perth Institute of Contemporary Art.

One of the many inspiring moments of the weekend was certainly Margaret Williams' (University of NSW) interview with Playworks' patron, Dorothy Hewett, an invigorating and intimate event that brought the full house to its feet, and Dorothy Hewett and many in the audience to tears. All we can do is plead insanity for failing to tape the session. The festival placed pressures on our resources and in an event based largely on papers, we neglected to organise a tape recorder for this live session. As soon as we realised our mistake, a few of us started madly scribbling notes in the dark and we've tried to make up for our oversight by putting these together for this book. For more detailed information, we recommend Margaret Williams' excellent critical analysis in *Dorothy Hewett: The Feminine as Subversion* (Currency Press). For those who were present the experience was unforgettable.

I don't know where to begin in thanking (Playworks) ....
To be part of the audience that gave the standing ovation to Dorothy Hewett, and afterwards to have the chance to say as there may not be another time to say it, thank you Dorothy - you made a difference - you showed us a way through ...

Suzanne Spunner , Northern Territory writer and director.

Another highlight was Angela Chaplin's account of travelling, talking and writing with Ningali Lawford whose solo performance in three languages (*Ningali*) has successfully toured Australia and the Edinburgh Festival, Berlin and London. Ningali had gone home to Broome and couldn't be coaxed to the city for our festival but it was good to hear Angela speaking about the collaboration between herself, Ningali and Robyn Archer on the making/writing of this work and, thanks to ABC TV, to see some of Ningali's performance on video. This and many other sessions during the weekend drew attention to the range of writing processes being used by Australian women performance writers.

Eighty-five delegates registered for *Playing With Time* from all over Australia. Many more attended day and half-day sessions. Interestingly, the sessions that filled the theatre were *The B File* and the Dorothy Hewett interview. We were pleased with the audience mix— which included academics, theatre writers, contemporary performance makers and other writers from around Australia. Most of the audience was female.

The unconventional format was generally felt to be a big success. It produced some wonderfully creative writing which you'll see from these papers and it was refreshing to hear writers speaking about their own writing over time—such reflection is usually reserved for academics, critics and historians. The event brought all of these together in a performative environment.

Of course, there were problems and disagreements. In a program designed to give as many writers the opportunity to speak, question-time was disappointingly limited for some. Although we didn't necessarily use a state-of-origin approach to the programming (many writers work across state borders) we did attempt a national profile. However, some very important people were left out. Western Australia was under-represented. Despite our efforts to include Queensland writers such as Elaine Acworth, Jill Shearer and Hilary Beaton, in the end none could attend and we were left with no Queensland representation at a very exciting time for women writers there.

> *My beef about Queensland representation represents something much larger.*
> *In the Australian theatre consciousness it's my perception that Queensland hardly rates.*
> *For years it's been considered a cultural joke, all boardshorts and pineapples.*
> *But, as you vigorously said, there is a great deal of positive work happening now and*
> *what we suffer from is poor marketing and invisibility (a bit like women writers really).*
> *For this reason, I've decided to start jumping up and down every time we're left out.*

Sue Rider, La Boite Theatre .

Some sessions were contentious (*The B File* and for some, the presentation of new works from the Playworks program in excerpt rather than as full-scale readings). Playworks operates with a staff of two, a committee of eight and a moving population of volunteers. Organising a major event like a festival along with a national workshop program and a major publication stretched our resources to the limit. Nevertheless we appreciated the constructive comments made by all who spoke up at the final session.

At the International Women Playwrights' Conference last year the focus was understandably on a range of important issues and the lineup of international guests. For many of us there was also a complementary function in meeting Australian writers, some for the first time. *Playing With Time* offered a rare opportunity for the community of Australian women writers to get together.

> *A weekend of honesty, commitment, careful thought, inspiration, joy.*
> *Women of confidence, women with something to say,*
> *women who are daring to speak, women who are wanting to listen—*
> *and women who are prepared to put in a great deal of time to make it happen!*

Sue Rider

> *The chance for me of catching up with old mates...*
> *to meet up again with ones I'm just beginning to know...*
> *to meet people I felt I knew but didn't in fact ...*
> *to meet up with people I'd forgotten I knew ...*
> *to be part of sharing so much history and experience was fantastic.*
> *As I have been so far away for more or less the whole decade,*
> *it was fantastic for me just to even see and hear some snippets—*
> *notwithstanding good, bad or indifferent videos—*
> *of some people's work who it has driven me to distraction*

that I haven't been able to see in the flesh—
I cannot tell you how valuable that was for me.
Over this time I've missed so much work I would have given anything to have seen.
After the weekend I feel a bit more filled in.

Suzanne Spunner

Women's writing for theatre is not an area I have thought a lot about.
I came to find out what's happening.
I went away knowing much more than when I arrived.
So in that sense, it worked as a festival,
an event offering a range of tastes. Each session was highly
structured but it didn't feel programatic.

Rachel Fensham, Monash University.

I enjoyed what I witnessed of your impressive conference,
particularly the great presence of Dorothy Hewett,
and I was inspired by this opportunity to get an idea of the forms women writers are
engaged with in contemporary Australia.
I feel I've returned to the UK much enriched with some of the debates and
concerns artists are engaged with.

Deborah Levy

Suzanne Spunner has the last word:

And on a totally personal neurotic note—
it was cheering in a perverse sort of way to be reminded that
writers are all as mad as cut snakes and as insecure,
and batty as each other, no matter how inexperienced, successful,
together we all appear to each other to be ...
I think this is one of the most valuable aspects of conferring with peers.

I liked the way you made it AN EVENT and
the thought and care that went into creative detailing ...

Because such opportunities to get together are rare, writers make the most of them.
Contacts were made at *Playing With Time*, ideas generated and hopefully there will be
many spin-offs, possibly in the form of future collaborations and in other such events in
the not too distant future.

The text and images in *Telling Time* make very good reading, recording as they do
in personal diaries of the decade reflections on the variety of motivations, processes,
interruptions to and conceptions of writing for performance by Australian women writers.

friday

07:45 PM

13:10:1995

0 KODAK 5053 TMY 11 KODAK 5053 TMY

0 KODAK 5053 TMY 11 KODAK 5053 TMY

introduction

virginia baxter

W elcome to *Playing With Time* a festival in thirty-two acts featuring the work of
Alma de Groen, Ningali Lawford and Tes Lyssiotis and the realtime real life
presences of in alphabetical order Paula Abood,
May-Brit Akerholt,
Andrea Aloise,
Virginia Baxter,
Sarah Brill,
Katharine Brisbane,
Susie Bromfield,
Angela Chaplin,
Jennifer Compton,
Cathy Craigie,
Megan Elliott,
Catherine Fargher,
Anni Finsterer,
Margaret Fischer,
Venetia Gillot,
Jane Goodall,
Regina Heilmann,
Nikki Heywood,
Dorothy Hewett,
Mary Hutchison,
Sue Ingleton,
Jenny Kemp,
Noëlle Janaczewska,
Tobsha Learner,
Deborah Leiser,
Deborah Levy,
Jacquie Lo,
Julie-Anne Long,
Alison Lyssa,
Sarah Miller,
Pamela Payne,
Deborah Pollard,
Melissa Reeves,
Victoria Spence,
Amanda Stewart,
Imogen Stubbs,
Peta Tait,
Yana Taylor,
Katherine Thomson,
Alana Valentine,
Terry Whitebeach,
Fiona Winning.

Playing With Time celebrates ten years of Playworks and is, like the organisation itself, performative. Since inception, Playworks has been an organisation for practitioners run by practitioners with help from the Australia Council and the NSW Ministry for the Arts. It is a small organisation with an ambitious program and this event would have to be one of our toughest acts so far, encompassing as it does a festival of writers, an intensive workshop with ten artists working with visiting writer Deborah Levy with further workshops in Melbourne and Brisbane, a major national survey of writers for theatre and performance culminating in a substantial publication — *Playing With Time: Women Writers for Performance*.

When I tried to come up with a performative metaphor for Playworks' experience in organising such an event, the closest I could get was a Chinese plate-spinning act. Some who have spun more than their share of plates include Colleen Chesterman who has given enormous energy to the collating and editing of the survey. Our administrator Caitlin Newton-Broad who I notice in her biog calls herself "a dedicated spectator", which I take to mean fully involved in all aspects of the performance which is exactly what she is. Designer and production manager Michelle Dado not only had to see to the plates but everything holding them up. And Clare Grant, co-director of Playworks and of the Festival who has been supervising proceedings between takes on the *Island of Dr. Moreau* where she has been playing the many-breasted fox lady with Marlon Brando. Thanks to Francesca Smith and the Playworks Committee (Margaret Williams, Jennifer Compton, Colleen Chesterman, Jacquie Lo, Noëlle Janaczewska, Alison Lyssa, Marion Potts, Anna Messariti, Helen Swan), Rosemary Cameron, Sally Richardson and the many individuals and organisations who have contributed to this project, especially the Centre for Performance Studies at Sydney University, The Performance Space, Sydney Theatre Company's New Stages, ABC Radio National, Keith Gallasch and *RealTime*, ABC TV's *Review*, SBS Independent, the State Library of NSW who have kindly loaned us slides from *The Work of Art: Australian Women Writers and Artists* exhibition, Leong Chan and the Design Department of the College of Fine Arts and many others like Crawfords who rang one day and said, "Sure we'd like to help. We'll pay for a writer to come — just tell us her name." (It was Margaret Fischer from South Australia).

Jennifer Compton, winner of the 1995 NSW Writers Fellowship, has counselled me against saying too many thank-yous. Just say to the others "You know who you are". And then she slipped me a fresh poem to fill the space. Something to add just the right degree of tension to a plate spinning act on Friday the 13th. It's called *Performance*.

The subtle smile of the saboteur
is pulling the crazy strings
She is rolling up the afternoon
running down insinuating stairs
flowering into the evening
The chairs won't stand for it

the script flies into a rage
the metaphysical sugar bowl
begins to tremble on the page
She smiles and smiles
an eyebrow raised
she answers to my own name
vanishes backstage.

... where I hope she stays for the rest of the weekend which we hope you'll enjoy in celebration of Playworks' first decade and all Australian women's writing for theatre and performance into the next.

One of the major projects of this celebration has been the publication of our survey of ten years of Australian women's writing for theatre and performance. The results of this survey are exhilarating in the volume and range of women's writing, but also alarming in their indication of the paucity of production of works by women writers on the mainstage and its smaller equivalents. This survey would not have been possible without the assistance of the Women's Grants Program of the NSW Department for Women that allowed us to survey writers in NSW. Later we were able to extend the survey to cover other states through the generosity of the Strategy and Communications Unit of the Australia Council. I have pleasure in inviting first Caroline Block, Director General of the NSW Department for Women and secondly Sarah Gardiner, Acting Head of Strategy and Communications Branch to launch *Playing With Time.*

Virginia Baxter
Chair of PLAYWORKS

14   KODAK 5053 TMY   15   K

14   KODAK 5053 TMY   15   K

the b-file

deborah levy

As part of the Festival, Playworks invited leading British writer of experimental performance, fiction and poetry, Deborah Levy to Australia to conduct workshops in Melbourne, Sydney and Brisbane. Deborah has written plays *(Pax, Clam* and *Heresies)* and her recent work for performance includes *Call Blue Jane* for ManAct Theatre, *The B-File* (originally commissioned by the European Arts Festival), *Shiny Nylon* with installation artist, Anya Gallacia. Her most recent performance work, *Honey Baby: Thirteen Studies in Exile* was produced by Suzanne Chaundy at La Mama Theatre in Melbourne to coincide with Deborah's visit for our festival. She has written novels *(Beautiful Mutants* and *Swallowing Geography)* and volumes of poetry *(An Amorous Discourse in the Suburbs of Hell* and *The Unloved)*. In 1991 she adapted the libretto from Lorca's *Blood Wedding* for composer Nicholas Lefanu. She has also edited an anthology, *Walking on Water* which features significant postmodern texts by experimental writers.

The workshop in Sydney involved eleven artists (Deborah Leiser, Terry Whitebeach, Fiona Winning, Regina Heilmann, Victoria Spence, Megan Elliott, Yana Taylor, Julie-Anne Long, Imogen Stubbs, Catherine Fargher, Venetia Gillot) from all over Australia and representing a range of performance practices (dance theatre, community theatre, performance poetry, spoken word and physically based performance). The two-week workshop became a rehearsal for a performance with participants contributing their own writing to the existing framework for *The B-File*, beginning with a set of questions about identity which interrogate both performers and audience.

Q: Is Beatrice an Australian character?
Q: If she is a character, is she dressed for the part?
Q: Is Beatrice a persona?
Q: If she is a persona what are her voices?

Further questions involved an imaginary lover. Each participant answered these questions in her own way, for example:

Julie-Anne Long

Q: Do you love X?
A: (divert eyes)
Q: Does X love you?
A: (Sing) When will I see you again,
       when will we shhhhhhhhh(finger to lips)
Q: What words do you say to X when you make love?
A: Stay down scrummy and show me y'tonsils.
Q: What effect do you want your words to have?
A: Supremacy.
Q: After you've made love who goes to sleep first?
A: Second (point to yourself)

Q: What do you think about while X sleeps?

A: Sheep. I think about sheep. Why do New Zealanders lay sheep on their backs when they make love to them?... So they can kiss them on the lips.

Fiona Winning

Q: Do you love X?
A: Sometimes.
Q: Does X love you?
A: Of course.
Q: What words do you say to X when you make love?
A: (exaggerating/lengthening the consonants) FFffellafel, spano-kop-ita, cus-tard, pa-pa-ya.
Q: What effect do you want your words to have?
A: Gluttony.
Q: After you've made love, who goes to sleep first?
A: Whoever's worked harder.
Q: What do you think about while X sleeps?
A: I think of swimming in champagne pools lined with rock oysters.... lifting their lids with my knife, being careful not to pierce the precious flesh inside. I suck the oysters from their shells and wonder why I always swim alone. Just me and my oyster knife.

Other participants were invited to write longer monologues.

Megan Elliott

Walgett. Largest wheat silo in Australia mate.
Walgett. You can see the black stump from here.
Walgett. A half horse town with more two bit mongrels than men.

Girl Guides and then Beatrice found God. A month of Sundays in one bloody afternoon. An absolute shitfight when she joined. Her old man reckoned she wasn't quite the full quid. She got the white frock though. White for virgin. Fuckin' fair suck of the sauce bottle mate–Beatrice was 13.

About as popular as a pork chop in a Synagogue: Beatrice in the Bush.

Beatrice's goal has always been to sleep next to a man who reckons that the three little words, "you awake luv?" will send her into a writhing, screaming, heaving, sweaty mass of not only multiple but simultaneous orgasms every Tuesday at 6.30 am.

Beatrice feeds the man meat, marries a bloke who goes to the pub with his mates, comes home pissed to the eyeballs, bashes Beatrice and the 2.2 kids, orders chops and three veg for tea, plus sweets, every night, except Sundays when it's a roast. Roast beef for real men, not that faggots' food, chicken.

Beatrice Ban the Books.
Beatrice Ban the Bomb.
Beatrice Bring out the Booze.

Beatrice. Two Mills and Boon every Christmas, before breakfast.

Chapter 1: This is what I want, he whispers, his long fingers kneading her, drawing a large arc over her engorged flesh. She was made for his arms, fitting them perfectly. His mouth plunders hers. His thumbs begin a slow sliding rotation of her nipples.

But it is Barthes, Roland Barthes, French philosopher and semiologist who suckles Beatrice as she sleeps.

R: Oh Beatrice. Mon petite choux. Mon amour. Oh Beatrice, oh la la Beatrice.
B: Oh Roland, oh Rolly, you're blood hot stuff Rolly.
R: Mon Chat, Mon Coeur, Mon Dieu. Je t'adore Beatrice. Everything follows from this principle: that the lover is not to be reduced to a simple, symptomal subject, but rather that we hear in her voice Beatrice, what is unreal.
B: Oh Barthes, make me howl like a stuck pig Bazza.
R: Oh Beatrice., I adore your propensity to talk with such repressed feeling, language is a skin, non? I rub my language against yours, it is as if I have words instead of fingers, or fingers at the tips of my words. My language trembles with desire.

And then Beatrice says: With you, my ute and my dog, I'm as happy as a pig in shit.

B: Beatrice, there is no metalanguage.

No. But there's Anzac Day and a Chinese Restaurant. Monthly shopping trips to Dubbo—a definite highlight. There's washing, ironing, Valium, Serepax, Mercyndol and Mogodon. There's Saturday nights at the RSL, Sundays at one of X's mates' place, where the men gather round the barbie, too pissed to know the difference between charcoal and chargrilled, while Beatrice sits with the other women, slowly getting off her tits as she washes down her pills and the blackened lumps of (rump was it?) with Fruity Lexia, ignoring the slaps on the arse from the other husbands. Beatrice doesn't see the point of exchanging one premature ejaculation for another.

Beatrice: I cut my teeth on twist tops, theology and the theories of choice.
*   Voulez vous coucher avec moi, ce soir?*

Terry Whitebeach, three weeks after the event, wrote from NT: ..."42 degrees and the red dust blowing and I abandon my prepared workshop, "Story of Truth–Truth Speaking as a way of confronting marginalisation, racism" and we have BEATRICE IN THE BUSH. The women really got off on old B—so we did "Look at me" Kimberley style and instead of "OMO, Shell, Meadowlea" we sang "A frog went walking and he did go ..." and at night the Warnum (Turkey Creek) women painted up and sang corroboree–fire dance: funniest sight of the weekend—an old desert woman, long breasted, swollen stomached–across her T-shirt breasts–"Calvin Klein". So we did Beatrice's journey and Beatrice's voices and Beatrice goes to Balgo (via Halls Creek, the Canning Stock Route and Well 33) and had a great time.

I am a writer and so the gains to me are counted mostly in terms of writing and those were oblique rather than direct–a whole host of sensual memories–sights, sounds of dancers, performers–and the dialogue in my own mind when "Beatrice" did not feel authentic and "Sandra" spontaneously erupted and began a complex dance with her European counterpart."

09:15 PM

the conversation continues

saturday

09:45 AM

14:10:1995

SATURDAY BEGINS WITH ROSE SHELLEY
(A CHARACTER FROM THE 20 MINUTE MONOLOGUE INVISIBLE SUN BY ALMA DE GROEN)
STANDING IN FOR THE PLAYWRIGHT HERSELF:

I've never enjoyed looking back, and when I tried to in this case (and I did try many times!)
much of my theatre history seemed like a form of aversion therapy. The only way to keep
writing is not to look back, otherwise I'd stop dead in my tracks. There were some wonderful
experiences with extraordinary people, but too much of the time I was the bad fairy at the christening
("Oh, God, not the writer again!)

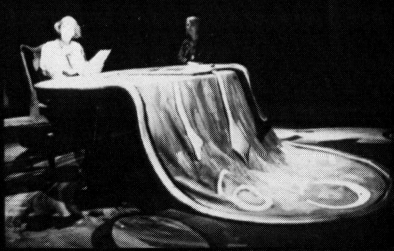

invisible sun

alma de groen

ALMA DE GROEN SENT A COPY OF INVISIBLE SUN
WHICH SHE INTENDED AS THE FIRST ACT OF A STAGE PLAY ENTITLED AVAILABLE LIGHT.
*WE THOUGHT IT APPROPRIATE TO OPEN THE CONFERENCE WITH THIS ONE ACT
FROM ONE OF AUSTRALIA'S MOST ADVENTUROUS PLAYWRIGHTS.
THE ROLE OF ROSE SHELLEY WAS READ BY JUDY FARR. HERE'S AN EXCERPT FROM THE WORK.*

*TIMEKEEPER, COLLEEN CHESTERMAN READ THE FOLLOWING ANNOUNCEMENT
AND PASSED THE TIME BY DISCREETLY TAKING NOTES THROUGHOUT THE READING
WITH TWENTY PENCILS.*

Our first speaker is Rose Shelley, one of Australia's leading women poets whose work
has recently been undergoing a revival.

Rose: Thank you for that flattering introduction—although I should point out that your
description of me as "one of Australia's leading women poets" was a little unnecessary.
Just "poet" will do. It's evident even at my age that I'm a woman. At least I hope it is.

SHE POURS HERSELF A GLASS OF WINE.

One of the penalties of age—the drop in the quality of the wine. I'm strictly cask variety
now, so this is a treat. I'll just have a final glass to remember it by ...

... Now. You want me to talk about myself and my work. That's difficult at present—for
reasons I probably shouldn't go into.

You may find this difficult to understand, since talking is something you do as academics.
But you talk about other people's work: you don't have to talk about yourselves. And you
have ideas you can hide behind. Including other people's. You're not exposed the way
a poet is. The poet is naked before you ... At least that's the way it feels standing up here
with everybody ... well never mind—
DRINKS

So, I'm going to follow your example. I won't just talk about Rose Shelley. I'll summon
another presence—a higher authority. In other words, I'll hide behind someone else.

I don't know if any of you read Sir Thomas Brown any more. Sir Thomas was one of my
mentors. You can make a note of that if you like: I'm trying to think of ideas that might be
relevant to English tutors dealing with my work—but since I don't know what's relevant to

it any more, that's something of a problem. And I hate dwelling on the past. I like to look ahead. Especially since I've been assured that I have another twenty years in which to do so. As Sir Thomas said in ... I think it was "Urn Burial"

"If the nearness of our last necessity, brought a nearer conformity unto it, there were a happiness in hoary hairs, and no calamity in half senses. But the long habit of living indisposes us for dying."

I read "Religio Medici" and "Urn Burial" when I was sixteen, and they were of such a beauty ... "Life is a pure flame, and we live by an invisible sun within us" ... Now, at sixty-seven, I know about the pure flame, and I know something about the half senses too.

DRINKS

There's some noble rot involved in this ...

A FURTHER TEST

Delicious.
In the words of Sir Thomas, "Who knows the fate of his bones, or how often he is to be buried?" It seems I was taken from my urn and my ashes spread abroad and re-examined. The verdict? "Rose Shelley is in the unique position of a poet who was dropped and now needs to be picked up again."

Astonishing. You dropped me, and I didn't know! If I fell through space, other than by my own volition, I was unaware of it!

And now you have picked me up again.

DRINKS

Do you know what it is to drop? ... Really drop? ... Falling helplessly, endlessly, out of the sky, like the air hostess in that terrifying poem by James Dickey? You might want to make a note of that—James Dickey: a poem called "Falling".

I wrote a poem. A long poem. I don't need to qualify that. We poets know when the machinery's in order. Presumably that's when you retrieved me after my unsuspecting drop. One has a life to lead, you know—hoping not to run out of typewriter ribbon before pension day—so we're not always au fait with our current standing in the charts.

My current standing with myself I'm always au fait with. When it comes to being dropped, no one does as good a job on me as I do.

SHE POURS HERSELF MORE WINE.

I dropped, as I said, endlessly ... And then I picked myself up. And, when it seemed I was all right again, I cracked, as Scott Fitzgerald said, "like an old plate".

I wrote poetry because that was how I planned to communicate. The rest could be "I'll have a dozen eggs, please, and some butter." I wanted to be in another time and place. I wanted it from childhood, with a longing that was physical—as if I'd been shut out from home. But home, the home I wanted, was an unknown place ... And when I found it, it wasn't somewhere outside me, it was inside. But I couldn't always gain access. Ninety-five per cent of the time I was shut out. And then I sat outside the door and howled like a dog.

DRINKS

I felt guilt. They say women feel this anyway; that it gives them a sense of importance in the world—that their actions matter enough that they could have something to feel guilty about. I felt guilt when I heard the news. Any news. Or when I read the news. Any news. It's always bad ...

Guilt. What was I doing, with this common Fire almost upon us, writing poetry that took longer and longer to come out—better each time when it did—but taking so long that between-times one had to be considered defunct. Dropped.

... In my forties it became all too obvious, and I never quite grew used to it: my lack of authenticity as a female. For most of our lives we're the genuine article. Then one day our provenance is questioned and we're declared fake. Quietly, of course. We're still there on the wall, but not looked at in the same way. If at all. At the slightest excuse we'll be thrown out and replaced with a real work of art.

Poetry was my protection. My racket. My criminal excess ...

Then one Friday night in Oxford Street about a year ago I caught a cab. The driver said "Would you like me to tell you how you can move through time and space?"

"I can do that already," I said, "I'm a poet. Slow down." The plate had already cracked. The driver had a friend. The friend conducted seminars. The first was free.

POURS MORE WINE

So much has opened up for me—because I hailed a taxi on a rainy night.

...We were told, all of us who were there, that whatever occupation we currently held, it would no longer be part of our lives. If we could not accept this we were to leave right then. A few people, who I imagined might be lawyers or in real estate, left. I was in my smashed plate phase so I stayed.

From Alma de Groen's *Available Light*.

THE FICTIONAL ROSE IS REPLACED BY THE REAL KATHERINE THOMSON,
A STACK OF RECOLLECTIONS FALLING FROM THE PAGES OF HER NOTEBOOKS AND SCRIPTS.

reflections

katherine thomson

At the time I didn't realise that this address would be published, and unfortunately much of my speech was in the form of notes which makes it somewhat difficult to recall. But here goes.

Having been asked to reflect on my work over the past ten years, I've spent some time this week fishing out notebooks and plays that I haven't read for many years. Apart from my two published works *Barmaids* and *Diving for Pearls,* the others are prompt copies covered in last minute changes, stage manager's notes and tagged at various places with re-writes particular to a given production.

The collection of opening night souvenir theatre stubs and thank you cards from the actors and director remind one of what a fleeting exercise it is.

My noticeboard, however, like those of most writers, has been a constant with two yellowing pieces of paper pinned there as reminders of what I am actually doing at my desk every day.

The first is a quote from the poet Flecker:

That the function of art is not to change men's souls but to make them glad that they have one.

The other is a quote from Agnes de Mille:

There is a vitality, a life force, a quickening that is translated through you into action, and because there is only one you in all of time, this expression is unique. And if you block it, it will never exist through any sort of medium and be lost.

The whole world will not have it. It is not your business to determine how good it is, nor how valuable nor how it compares with other people's expressions. It is your business to keep it yours clearly and directly, to keep the channels open. You have to keep open and aware to the changes that motivate you ...

No artist is pleased ... There is only your divine dissatisfaction, a blessed unrest that keeps us marching, and makes us more alive than others."

To Agnes de Mille from Martha Graham and from Tommy Tune to us.

My reflection of the last ten years, which of course also means looking into the future, is composed of two elements—the work one has produced as well as the adjustments one makes to working as a writer. By this I mean the ongoing balances of confidence, faith in oneself, clarity required to work in a collaborative medium as well as the balancing of the isolation one needs in order to write, with "being in life" and allowing oneself to be immersed in the life experiences one needs to have something to write about.

Needless to say, a lot of the energy of being a writer also goes into the mental games one learns to play, rather like those of an actor; along with the internal adjustments to one's motivation or the techniques one develops to deal with both spoken and unspoken criticism from those who don't care for your work. Not to mention those who wish you would just stop, just *give up* so that the theatre can become a better place for all concerned. Particularly critics.

10:15 AM ━━━━━━━━━━━━━━━━━━━━▶interruption

LIGHT DOWN ON KATHERINE THOMSON,
LIGHT UP ON PAMELA PAYNE IN THE AUDITORIUM AND ON VIDEO MONITOR.

I'm always interested in the fact that the public understanding of most plays can come from two or more sources. In the first instance, there's the text. Anyone who has read, for example, *Diving For Pearls* can say: "Yes, I know what it's about—from my perspective". Their impression of the play, and of you as a writer, has come from their reading of the text. This is perhaps the most limited way of experiencing the play. And it's very much dependant on individual ability to read a script as a theatrical work. But in another sense, it's the purest, the least trammelled by outside influence.

Then there are all those—the majority—who see *Diving For Pearls* and go home saying: "Yes, we know Katherine Thomson's play; we've just seen it". This is, of course, the way every playwright wants her work to be experienced—on the stage. Nevertheless, the audience have not necessarily seen your play as you conceived it. They've seen it filtered through the creative intelligences of a director, designer and actors.

I've seen several productions of both *Barmaids* and *Diving For Pearls*. And each one has, of course, been different. Some productions might, in your eyes, have diminished your work. Others might have thrilled you—revealed things you barely knew were there. One sent me back to the script to see whether what I had just seen was the same play.

But the point is, whatever the production—fantastic, ordinary or awful—it lives in the memory as Katherine Thomson's play. There's nothing you or any writer can do about that—although it becomes less of an issue if audiences see more than one production.

Pamela Payne

Recently at the Australian Film TV and Radio School during the "Write Stuff" program, I was reminded of being in a position rather similar to this one today, where the very nature of sitting "out the front" confers a particular status on the speaker and, forgive me if any of you were at that session, but it prompted me to attempt to describe the kind of writer I am.

Two recent events encapsulate my state of mind. Recently I was near completion on a telefeature, at about the same time my computer blew up. Unable to afford a new one, I rented one for a month, the rental period expiring at about the time I was handing in my final draft. The internal conversation went something like, "Well... the draft's hopeless ... this'll be the one where I'll have to give up writing ... so throw out the computer brochures. I certainly won't be needing one of those." Needless to say, when the producers expressed admiration for the draft the world changed.

Similarly the internal monologue when one is in the middle of a draft that goes, "What a dreadful occupation this is, who'd be a writer, but my room is on the eleventh floor and all I'd have to do is open a wind ..." transforms once at least someone of influence expresses an interest in the work at hand. "What a marvellous job to have! Who'd be anything but a writer! How privileged am I?"

But back to the projects of the last ten years, and the observations I made reaching into the archive boxes—the very boxes one wishes one could drag into rehearsal as people sit with your one hundred pages before them, wishing you could say "Look at these four archive boxes'. *That's* where this has come from! Look at all this work."

I'm often reminded when finishing a project, of the author of *Whose Life Is it Anyway?* Brian Clarke. As he was writing this he thought, "This is going to be it. This is going to be epic. This is going to be the big one." He finished it, drew a line under it, read it and thought: "Ah sod it. It's me again."

I feel neither qualified, nor capable of distinguishing a pattern in the style of my work. Many of you present were no doubt recipients of a survey by a PhD student, asking writers to define our plays within a multiple choice list of style—realistic, naturalistic, naturo-realistic etc. Most people I know didn't complete the form as requested. The definitions are for others to place, not for us to define.

So what indeed is the value of writers talking about writing anyway? I recall two writers' sessions over the past ten years which have had shored me up ready to face my desk the next day. One was Mary O'Malley at an Australian Film TV and Radio School talk one Sunday afternoon, in the middle of a lot of male writers all lamenting the fact that the swag of fab ideas that they have for this or that are ignored in favour of commercial dross. Mary O'Malley stood up to speak, and for the first time in my life I heard a writer admit that she doesn't have a trailer full of ideas, that ideas are not easy to come by, and so when she does have one, she hangs onto it with some ferocity.

Similarly Tom Stoppard who said that he always thinks that the last play he wrote was indeed his last. And then three or four years roll by ... and an idea starts to niggle ...

Having said that, I am rather aware of the set-up, and am not meaning to suggest that I am going to provide any gob-smacking gems today ...

I asked myself what I look for when deciding on what to write for the theatre. Something I know I'm going to be passionate about for the next x months or years; something that starts to disturb my unconscious, and most importantly something that is worthy (in my mind anyway) of that arena, that space.

Perhaps it's worth confessing publicly that I'm an optimist, that I have great faith that is continually being borne out, in the ability of human beings to change. To transform themselves. But having said that, in part I think I write from anger —increasingly so in the past five years—that we don't find it easy to tell the truth, either privately or publicly, and that we increasingly seem to operate from fear.

All of which is starting to sound like the stuff of conscientious drama whereas, in part, the responsibility of the theatre is to unbalance, to provoke change in the hearts of the audience. Which brings us to another problem. Change is rather a double-edged sword in the 90's. What was once the domain of radicalism and *ipso facto* good theatre, is now common sense. Change happens quickly, people's attitudes go through pretty astonishing reversal so that the most many of us can hope for is to keep track of change.

But theatre must do more than just 'plug in', even though I admire the writers who do just that. But in terms of what I need to motivate me to write for the theatre ... it's more to do than just holding our heads down as writers and munching on the domestic—the curse of so much American theatre. Some Italian writers visited the Writers' Forum at the STC this year and commented that change was happening so swiftly, that politics was leaping about so much, that it was like being under a tidal wave. One couldn't be sure whether one was in the middle of it, the end of it, or the beginning of it. But most importantly it was impossible to know who had started it. They felt that the atrophy of their playwrights and theatre reflected this conundrum.

So back to me hoping to write another play, within the context outlined above. The reason that I haven't done so over the last two years is a personal one, until recently I've woken at 3 am to the internal chant of, "When are you going to start your play?"— a little like the American TV commercial "It's 11 pm. Do you know where your children are?"

I observe, in reading through *Change in the Weather* and *Tonight We Anchor in Twofold Bay* to *A Sporting Chance* to *Darlinghurst Nights* and ending with *Diving for Pearls,* a gradual progression from what might be called vertical to linear structure, if one takes as a definition of the former a situation in which the characters and their actions don't affect the drama so much as reflect it. They're observers to the action of the play. Being rather than doing is stressed. Conflict exposes ideas, attitudes and dreams within an orchestrated tension ...

Diving for Pearls, which came out of a combination of a desire of mine to write a play about my coal-mining cousins, and a research job with ABC documentaries on Wollongong, was enhanced by discussions with Paul Thompson on narrative structure, and of course, the dramaturgical support of Playworks after the first draft.

In terms of *Barmaids* I sincerely wish I had had similar support. As it was, I had to do the lot on my own, and sorely missed any kind of dramaturgical or directorial contribution to the process.

10:25 AM   interruption

AT THIS POINT THE PHONE ON THE TABLE RINGS.
ANGELA CHAPLIN IS ON THE MOBILE PHONE IN THE AUDIENCE.
SHE IS CAUGHT BY THE VIDEO CAMERA.

AC   *Kath, Hi!*

KT   *Hi Angela. where are you?*

AC   *Never mind where I am,*
      I hear you've been bad-mouthing me at the festival in Sydney.

KATHERINE DENIES ANY BAD-MOUTHING AND INVITES ANGELA ON STAGE
WHERE THE TWO SPEAK ABOUT THEIR COLLABORATIONS.
THERE ARE NO NOTES PREPARED,
BUT THE ESSENCE OF THE CONVERSATION IS THAT
THEY ARE A MUTUAL ADMIRATION SOCIETY,
ALWAYS LOOKING TO FIND WAYS OF WORKING TOGETHER.

survival

tobsha learner

I don't want to give a potted history of the works of Tobsha Learner, neither do I want to give an embittered diatribe about the limitations of the industry, the difficulty of being produced in Sydney or what it's like to worry about superannuation after years of freelancing ...

I thought I'd talk about survival. Personal survival: What keeps us going, for me, as it is for most of you, is still the dialogue with the audience, being an emotional catalyst for large groups of people, sitting in the dark, feeling their reactions, the fear, the trepidation, the dialogue of live theatre that film, television and radio cannot offer.

So if that keeps me going, obviously it's important to be produced...to stay unproduced is often the death knell of the playwright, or at least a major factor towards mental and emotional instability in a precarious and fickle microcosm called the Australian theatre industry which, frankly, has little or nothing to do with the support and or promotion of new talent and everything to do with balancing the books, filling the auditorium and perpetuating the status quo.

Therefore, it is important to seek production aggressively, whether it means producing your own work, seeking production out on the fringe, or deliberately tailoring your work for mainstream production houses. It is essential for the playwright to go through the production process. No amount of workshopping will give you the same working insight, the same dialogue with an audience of real people (as opposed to industry personnel) as going through your first season.

Which brings me to the importance of a second season. With some of my plays I have had the fortune to have had several seasons; some of the larger works have had successful seasons but have not being picked up for second seasons. Second seasons are essential for the development of all elements of the play, the physicality, dramaturgy, characterisation, what works with an audience, what doesn't. Far too many new works appear and disappear like tragic shooting stars, never to have the chance to continue to evolve ...

This creates a transitory, quick-fix culture involving a constant turnover of one hit wonders that never have a chance to settle down and develop into future Australian classics. Developing plays takes a great deal of time, commitment, money and courage ... With a few notable exceptions, I see little of it around me.

Increasingly, theatre companies are turning to revivals, one-handers about famous people or this year's slant on *Hamlet*. It's a vicious cycle; unless you create a market for new works you cannot fill the subscriber season, but you cannot create a market place without polished product and polished product involves time, money and risk. And if anyone knows of a theatre company which has those to spare, let me know afterwards ...

Survival: I think it is essential to carve a persona out for oneself within the theatrical community to stay viable, to remain a vital force within that field. This requires a great deal of stamina, egotism and naivety. The naivety is hard to hang onto, the stamina you can buy at the bar and the egotism is inherent.

The only way to maintain a persona is to stay produced. Over the last ten years in one way or another I have managed to do this, but then I'm an aggressive little bugger who won't go away. You have to stay real, and expect your spirit to be broken over and over and over again and then again. And then find the naivety to stand up and keep fighting.

It is unrealistic and simplistic to expect to write a play then sell it to a production house. Increasingly, production houses have their own artistic and financial criteria as well as their own commissions set up which also have absolutely no guarantee of production. Target your production house, research the demographic, write for under six characters, throw a wallop of sex in there, pepper the tragedy with comedy, seduce the artistic director and you might get read by the in-house dramaturg and not the receptionist.

How I survive: I have an audience, in some parts of the country people actually know the name. That helps. Not much, but it helps. I also, like most of the writers in this forum, write for many different mediums, this helps cover the telephone bill, and in some instances skills spill over into different fields. For example writing for radio, I believe, improves my screen writing, and writing for film influences my use of light and sound in theatre ...

Recently I've moved into directing; not because I was disillusioned with the directors I've worked with, far from it, I truly believe in theatre as a collective process. I moved into directing because (a) eight hours a day in front of the computer is extremely lonely and leads to fits of delusion; (b) I started as a sculptor and have always firmly believed in theatre being the physical space between people, like the silence between the lines; and (c) I wanted to see what I was like to work with as a playwright, then I could decide never to work with me again if I fucked up...

The play was a new work entitled *Seven Acts of Love (as witnessed by a cat)*, a sexy comedy that covered every social and sexual demographic I could think of bar pederasts ... Interestingly enough, we marketed it as such. It was, in fringe terms, a hit, we got a couple of embarrassingly laudatory reviews, a couple of vindictive ones (I dread the day I ever get a consensus of opinion) and word of mouth was very good ... And we broke even. It was ovary breaking, gut wrenching hard work, not helped by a complete lack of funding, back to shoe string facilities with a production staff that were exhausted, over-worked, obscenely paid, in other words your usual fringe venue.

However, the experience of dealing again with physical space, the actual carving out especially of the text, the tension between the actors, the choreography of those emotional journeys, re-enthused and reminded me why I got involved with theatre in the first place. I hope to continue to direct in the future. Directing does give you an insight into the limitations and potential of your own work. I've also discovered a whole new empathy for both directors and actors I have never had before.

Too many playwrights, and I can only speak from a narrative-based perspective, are alienated from the actual process of theatre itself. Some of them, I suspect, are more influenced by television than live theatre.

Survival: I feel obligated to talk about themes. Themes ... okay, I write about a broad variety of subjects in a variety of genres. *The Glass Mermaid*, which premiered last November at Playbox and was directed by Aubrey Mellor, was essentially a study in bereavement, about a middle-aged widow hiring a male escort to role play her dead husband, a kind of ritualising of grief.

The two protagonists, both having suffered bereavement, fall in love, so essentially it's a tragedy which has at its core a love story. I write about anything to do with sexuality, death, estranged migrants that have gone through an epic experience like war off shore and have ended up in comparative security in Australia—as in *Witchplay* where the central character is a Jewish medium who has survived the Holocaust, or the escort in *The Glass Mermaid* who is a Bosnian refugee, or in the radio play *Volkov* where the central character is a Russian cab driver who, as a violinist, fled Stalin.

In terms of actual process, I am increasingly drawn to the concept of light and sound and a very sparse set playing vital roles in both the tone and characterisation within the play. For example, through working closely with Rachel Bourke (who won a Green Room award for her lighting in *The Glass Mermaid*) and Aubrey and even through the development of the play with Keith Gallasch as dramaturg, I was determined that the lighting (having the light house beam sweep across the stage—and the division of natural time delineated by visible sunrises and sunsets) would play into the psychology of the play and help create a heightened naturalism, enabling me to explore esoteric things like the actual cry of the mermaid ... heard but not seen. As a director, and in my future scripts I want to go further into this area, and in my next stage production with Zootango entitled *The Bone King*, I'm bringing in a composer on first draft.

The importance of developing on-going relationships with crew and other directors is essential. Both Rachel Bourke and Stuart Mackenzie worked with me on *Seven Acts of Love (as witnessed by a cat)* after working on *The Glass Mermaid*. Through this dialogue it is possible to develop a short-hand and also enough trust to get honest feed-back during the actual process of shaping and rehearsing a play.

Finally, I believe it is essential for playwrights to get out there and converse with their audiences, to live a life not in the foyer or the launch or yet another matinee, but out in the streets, in many different sections of society because all we are, finally, are mirrors.

I'm now going to show a scene from *The Glass Mermaid*. This is the first time it has been seen outside of Victoria.

VIDEO: The Glass Mermaid

saturday

11:20 AM

14:10:1995

29   ▷ 29A   30   ▷ 3(

29   ▷ 29A   30   ▷ 3(

a dialogue with disjunction

jenny kemp

*TIMEKEEPER COLLEEN CHESTERMAN PLAYS PATIENCE AT THE TABLE.
JENNY KEMP STANDS AT THE MICROPHONE.
THROUGHOUT HER PRESENTATION,
SHE SHOWS VIDEO EXCERPTS FROM HER ELEGANT AND EVOCATIVE WORKS
(INCLUDING CALL OF THE WILD, SWEET DREAMS AND REMEMBER),
AGAIN, FOR MOST OF THE AUDIENCE
A TANTALISING TASTE OF WORK THEY ARE UNLIKELY TO HAVE SEEN OUTSIDE MELBOURNE.
THE GOOD NEWS IS THAT HER NEW WORK BLACK SEQUIN DRESS
WAS COMMISSIONED FOR THE 1996 ADELAIDE FESTIVAL.*

*I think our culture mistakenly thinks that knowledge and wisdom are the same things ...
Real growth comes in the feeling life, in the inner life, by being able to tolerate uncertainty
and ambiguity long enough to sustain oneself in doubt and uncertainty without an irritable
reaching for reason.*

Australian Jungian psychologist, Peter O'Connor

1. A FEELING OF DISJUNCTION

... as you walk down the street you see the *real* world but feel aware of an 'inner world'.
My work attempts a dialogue with this disjunction. Societal time frame often leaves us at
odds, or out of phase with ourselves and the world. This disjunction is uncomfortably
emphasised.

Oh god, am I late? I never have any time.

Consequently communication at a deeper level within the psyche is often not possible
and access to inner resources is cut off. This tight linear organisation of time amounts
to a political act of domination.

Based on the premise that any ordinary action has extraordinary resonances, the
intention is *to liberate the audience from the usual constraints of convention*, especially
those of time, and provoke *an imaginative and associative engagement with image and
text.* Memory, dream, fantasy, desire and myth are asked to play more active and
creative roles.

29

2. CONVENTIONAL THEATRE STRUCTURES

Our dramatic structures have for far too long simulated our society's social structures and its linear relationship to time which, while intending a critique, often results in reinforcing those structures and causing a cut-off point in the psyche of the audience.

I was originally a theatre director. However I found it hard to find plays that I wanted to direct. Thankfully this is now beginning to change, but it was one of the main reasons for my beginning to write. I also found an absence of texts which were expressing or prepared to explore the psyche enough.

3. DREAMS

I have always found dreams full of extraordinary information, always a source of wonder, and often guidance, and have tried to build into my life and work ways of listening to them. Also, the form of the dream has influenced my work. Firstly, the dream actually occurs simultaneously, not in a linear structure: only as we try to remember the dream do we organise it into beginning, middle and end. Secondly, a dream has a dreamer who often watches him/herself in the dream. I find it interesting to meditate on this relationship as parallel to the audience/performer relationship. The performance becomes the audience's dream.

4. MYTHS

Reading the *I Ching* and looking at myths has always informed my understanding of life patterns and structures and therefore helps my ability to construct a dramatic grid from my writing.

Some *real life* events that have influenced me:

5. VISUAL ARTS

My father was an abstract expressionist painter, and so I grew up looking into these frames. Mostly I notice that a painting of this nature removes all time constraints for and in the viewer. A painting is *static* and asks its viewer to *become active, internally active/meditative*. In conventional theatre forms, the performance is often active/often didactic and can cause its audience to become *too passive*. I want to stimulate a relationship between the performance and the audience which allows for a greater interplay between the active and passive possibilities of both. To this end, I feel it is essential to build a dramatic structure which disrupts conventional time frames/patterns.

I often use the paintings of the surrealist artist Paul Delvaux as an inspiration for the design and the mise en scène in my work. Because they always remind me that the world *on stage* is a timeless place, a kind of landscape of the psyche where anything can happen.

6. MENTAL ILLNESS

I have always had close relationships to people with mental illness and these have developed a strong desire in me to understand the inner world of the psyche more deeply and its connection to the everyday world.

7. CHOICE

In the end my work is perhaps the result of a choice to investigate the psyche and its ability to *function creatively.*

AS JENNY KEMP MOVES FROM THE MICROPHONE, NIKKI HEYWOOD MOVES THROUGH THE AUDIENCE.

saturday

11:35 AM

14:10:1995

9A 9A

10 10

10A 10A

jean / lucretia

nikki heywood

NIKKI HEYWOOD ENTERS THE THEATRE
SINGING FROM BENJAMIN BRITTEN'S THE RAPE OF LUCRETIA,
"SHE SLEEPS AS A ROSE UPON THE NIGHT".
SONG GIVES WAY TO VOICE-OVER
AS NIKKI'S BODY REMEMBERS HER GRANDMOTHER JEAN.

In creating this incomplete portrait of my grandmother,
I was aware that the feature of her life which was most compelling was her ordinariness.
In many ways her life began at the front gate and ended at the back fence.
Jean/Lucretia addresses those performance traditions such as opera
where it is more usual to celebrate characters
who are extraordinary, heroic or tragic, larger than life, and often in the case of women,
young and beautiful.
A challenge to see beauty in the dance of creaking old bones.
To see feeding the chickens as belonging to another kind of epic cycle.

Nikki Heywood

*THE CRUNCHING SOUND OF TWIGS IN DARKNESS. NIKKI HEYWOOD ENTERS CARRYING A
LARGE BUNDLE OF TWIGS. MUSIC. SHE IS DRESSED AS AN OLDER WOMAN. SHE WEARS A HAT
AND CARRIES A HANDBAG. AS SHE ENTERS SHE SINGS A VERSE FROM "SCHLUMMERLIED"
FROM THE RAPE OF LUCRETIA.*

SHE LAYS DOWN THE BUNDLE OF TWIGS, THEIR SHADOW CAUGHT BEHIND ON A SCREEN.

*PAUSE. MOVEMENT IN THE NEXT SECTION IS CONCENTRATED ON FEET, SHOES, LEGS,
THE PERFORMER'S MEMORY OF HOW HER GRANDMOTHER STOOD AND WALKED.*

TAPED VOICE:

*I have strong memories of my grandmother Jean's legs and feet. She wore pointy shoes
with a medium heel. Often beige coloured. At first I remembered her as being slightly
pigeon toed, but when I looked at a range of photographs of her, I saw she in fact often
stood with her feet open. More a duck-footed stance.*

PAUSE.

I can remember watching her standing in the kitchen with one foot resting on her knee. She'd just be balanced there on one foot. Chopping up beans. Making a cup of tea. And whenever she opened the kitchen cupboards she'd make sure you couldn't really see what was in there. She'd close them again very quickly.

PAUSE.

FROM HERE TWO VOICES CUT ACROSS EACH OTHER. MOVEMENT THROUGHOUT EXPLORES THE PHYSICAL MEMORY OF THE GRANDMOTHER'S BODY AND ITS MOVEMENTS.

VOICE 1	VOICE 2
She did an awful lot of walking.	*I remember going with her to Ramsgate Baths,*
She walked every day to the beach	*or Carr's Park Baths when I was a little girl.*
Down to the salt baths.	*And afterwards*
She walked to the library	*when we'd go into the changing room,*
She walked to the Blood Bank,	*just watching*
the Red Cross	*the other old ladies getting changed and*
	looking up seeing all these folds of flesh and
	this sagging skin and
	wondering how,
	how you could become like that.
She spent an awful lot of time	
out in the backyard,	
in the garden.	
I remember her hands.	*When she went to the Red Cross ..*
Tanned from the sun.	*(She was actually one of their oldest*
	serving members)
	she used to crochet these funny little dolls and
	coat hangers for their fêtes.
	For their stall.
	She raised a lot of money for the Red Cross.
	She was very proud of that.

FADE UP MUSIC: A CHEESY RENDITION OF "HUMORESQUE" BY DVORAK.

And right down at the bottom of the yard
was the chookpen.
When I was a child I'd sit entranced for hours.
Watching the chickens.
Sometimes I was allowed to feed them,
and I'd eat most of the pollard myself.

FADE MUSIC

As she got older,
my grandmother's feet,
her legs were afflicted with arthritis
and her feet and ankles just swelled up
so that her shoes left a mark on her feet.

And her hands ...
She was always fidgeting with her hands,
or with a hankie.

And her hands became
more and more contracted.

PAUSE.

Eventually, when she was in the hospital,
she'd stopped walking altogether
and she'd just spend hours sitting
in a chair in her room.
Gazing out the windows.
And she'd have to be lifted then
into her bed at night.
And then in the morning
they'd put her back into the bed
and then in the morning back into the chair
and then at night back into the bed
and then in the morning back into the chair
and then at night back into the bed
and then in the morning back into the chair
and back into the bed and back to the chair
and back into the bed,
until eventually she just stayed. In the bed.

I remember in the late afternoon
she'd stand there
in the garden with the hose.
She'd have one hand on her hip.
Spraying the garden.
And smell of the wet earth.

It all just seemed to be
one extension of her home.
Through from the front gate right out,
through the house where there were doilies
always on freshly dusted furniture
and the smell of lemon in the kitchen,
or cake —
freshly cooked cake —
out, down the back steps
past the laundry and the toilet
where she always had that sort of hard,
cheap, crinkly toilet paper,
and then out past the garden
and the chook pen.
And we'd stand on the back fence,
my brother and I
would stand on the back fence
and look out into the big paddock
over the fence
where there had been market gardens
but then it turned into a children's park.
And we'd try and imitate the chooks.

SHE ATTEMPTS AN IMITATION.

PAUSE

PAUSE

VOICE 1	**VOICE 2**

And her shoulder
had become particularly contracted,
so that her head   _You know those photos of the remains_
was sort of resting permanently on her shoulder.   _that they found in the peat bog?_
And her left arm was just pulled in.   _Well her body began assume that shape._
And I tried to massage   _It was all sort of flattened out_
and make her relax her shoulder   _and her skin was almost shiny._
which she would do just for a few moments   _Like the effect of the peat on those bodies._
but then as soon as I'd stop touching it
she'd lift it again.

Over the years,   _And, oh,_
before she went into hospital,   _the other thing was that her hands began,_
each time I visited the house   _as they contracted from_
the garden was being slowly transformed   _the arthritic condition,_
from the sort of lush paradise   _became very congested with blood._
with vines everywhere   _So the joints were thickened um ... and dark._
and flower beds and fish ponds, with concrete
so she wouldn't have to look after them any more
and then the flower beds just ended up
as a stretch of that harsh bladey grass.

And the vines came down off the fences.

And then she started on a beautiful olive tree
that was out in the front.
She started pruning away at that
and then began lopping the branches
and eventually she was just left
with the stump of the tree.
And when it still refused to die,   _And it just looked like_
she had to poison it.   _the blood flow had slowed_
     and eventually
     stopped altogether.
     And there's something about that
     that reminds me of the tree
     that she chopped down.
     ...sort of

petrified wood.

So the shininess of the skin of the bog body.

It's a lot like bark of an old tree which ...
oh ...
it reminds me of a frangipani tree
that was in the front garden too.
You know that skin on a frangipani tree,
the way it's hard and shiny.
Well her skin became like that, in the hospital.

And she just got smaller and smaller.

At her funeral
my aunt told me a story
about coming down the back yard
to find my grandmother ...
this was not long before
she went into the hospital,
and she couldn't bend down any more.
My aunt found her down there
with a walking stick
just poking a few little holes
into the dirt of the garden with the stick
and reaching into the apron pocket
and pulling out a couple of seeds.
I don't know what sort of seeds they were,
dropping the seeds into the holes
she'd made in the dirt
and just scraping the dirt back
over with her shoe.

MUSIC UP. SUNG LIVE VOICE.

AS NIKKI HEYWOOD MOVES ACROSS THE STAGE
HER SHADOW CROSSES SUE INGLETON ON HER WAY TO THE MICROPHONE.

saturday

12:30 PM

a grandmother, a cow,

14:10:1995

A LOUD BURST OF ANNIE GET YOUR GUN. *SUE INGLETON AT THE MICROPHONE.*

MUSIC FROM THE FILM ORLANDO

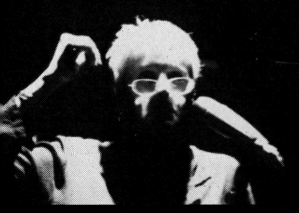

KODAK 5053 TMY   32   KODAK 5053 TMY   33

KODAK 5053 TMY   32   KODAK 5053 TMY   33

cannibal ants, fat ladies of the carousel, singing shells, angels and jesus

sue ingleton

I am moving down a slow river
the surface is mirror   tall cypress on either side
reflection   perfect
ahead   white light

I am moving down a black river
golden wheatfields on either side
the sky is grey, threatening   dark
the wheat glows   luminescent

I am at the bottom of a stone staircase
above me   in a black bubble
sits a white robed figure

I am watching a living cell divide
and divide
and divide

I am looking at my cunt
lips opening   dark crevice
soft flesh

My flesh opens   my cunt
is the rose window
in Chartres Cathedral

My cheek caresses the detail of carved curved stone

I am above my kitchen table   .
The lino needs a wash
The light is on.

MUSIC ENDS.

In this lifetime
from the cradle to the grave, in this lifetime
I'm a show-off.

So how did my soul cope with that?

YOU DO IT!
Oh Goodie.

In this lifetime, my star chart tells me
in this life,
I am a crusader.
I am a crusader and a show off
and when I was very very very young—

MUSIC: OVERTURE ANNIE GET YOUR GUN *FADING THROUGH NEXT SEGMENT.*

—my mother took me to see Evie Hayes in *Annie Get Your Gun*.

One hundred and thirty moons ago I was performing *Strip Jack Naked* to packed houses
in Edinburgh and London. The English papers called me the answer to Dame Edna.

There was a wide and definite path—it seemed.

Crusading like mad   people laughing.

Me dancing along the edges of my heart, the edges of my pain.

MUSIC ENDS.

One Summer later
I turned from the path—it seemed—and headed down a narrow little
track, like a vein of silver in a rock, like a vein of blood in my body.
Two more Winters and I held it in the palm of my hand.
Near Ms's. It was a gift, for me—for you.

Then the knocking started, the back door of my brain—the pressure

No More Reading! No More Thinking!, screamed my soul.

One more Spring

and this time there was no path
          just the void

the dark
the unknown

The Passion and its deep connection with lemon delicious pudding was coming through.

*I know that when I write there is something inside me which stops functioning,
something that becomes silent.
I let something take over inside me that probably flows from my femininity.
But everything shuts off
—the analytical way of thinking inculcated by college, studies, reading, experience.
It's as if I were returning to a wild country.*

Marguerite Duras

It's as if the universe takes my hand and dances my body through the keyhole of the text, my body becomes the key and I unlock the meaning of the text through it.

Two Autumns down—writing, writing ...
and I am just beginning to understand   to fit the jigsaw together.

The story is Silver's. There are mothers, fathers, aunts, sons and daughters, a grandmother, a cow, cannibal ants, fat ladies of the carousel, singing shells, angels and Jesus and lots lots more—births, death, murder and mayhem—sounds like cable television.

FROM HERE SUE IMPROVISED A CONVERSATION WITH THE AUDIENCE.

DOROTHY HEWETT IS SEATED ON STAGE WITH MARGARET WILLIAMS.
THE INTERVIEW IS NOT BEING RECORDED.
THE FOLLOWING NOTES ARE BEING COMPILED BY
ALISON LYSSA AND VIRGINIA BAXTER.
WHAT FOLLOWS IS FAIRLY CLOSE TO THE WORDS SPOKEN AS NOTED AT THE TIME.

it doesn't have to be a blood sport

dorothy hewett

Margaret Williams explains that when some of her students interviewed Dorothy Hewett recently, they were surprised to find she was 'not a dragon'. Why still this image? Clearly, Dorothy Hewett can still polarise both men and women. But all women playwrights, whether they feel an affinity with her work or not, owe Dorothy Hewett a debt as a trailblazer in the Australian theatre—not just for being a woman playwright (there had been others before her), or breaking into the mainstream but in claiming the right for women to write as they feel and about what they feel, whether it's socially acceptable or not.

Margaret asks Dorothy why she started writing for theatre relatively late. Dorothy speaks about the late 1960s when Australian theatre was stirring, how she watched what was going on, thinking to herself:

DH Even though you were female and years older than these spunky young males, you might be able to have some say in it. And it turned out that I did.

MW You're also a poet and novelist. What is it about theatre that keeps drawing you back to it?

DH Being commissioned, I think. I was too long in the tooth to sit around waiting for some director to pick up my play, not to mention a theatre company. I was 51 when my first play was put on. Writing plays in a vacuum is useless. Unless you're terribly lucky it just doesn't work. Unless you've got links with a theatre company or some other organisation that will put them on, you'll starve.

> *WA's Black Swan and Melbourne Theatre Company*
> *approached Dorothy recently to stage a work of hers.*
> *At first she refused saying, "Women get a rough trot ... Theatre is no place for a woman."*

DH Then they said, "What if we commissioned you? Would that change your mind?" I said "I'll think about it". I didn't want to sound too eager. I've written the first few scenes and the end. I can see daylight.

> *Dorothy talks about theatre companies who have always seen her as risky business.*
> *She explains that her relationship with the STC was briefly wonderful,*
> *but after a couple of plays—Mukinupin and Fields of Heaven*
> *—they did not continue to produce her work, or commission further work,*
> *or revive any of her earlier plays.*

DH Revivals have been few and far between. *The Chapel Perilous* has had one mainstage production. *This Old Man Came Rolling Home* which I wrote in 1968 had a production at the MTC in 1990. *The Man From Mukinupin* has been produced by all the State companies ... Without the student and occasional amateur productions, I'd be dead on the ground. I thought it would change when *Mukinupin* broke the then box office records at the STC, but it didn't.

MW You've said rightly that in other countries your work wouldn't be seen as particularly radical in terms of form, but Australian theatre still seems to have some trouble with plays that deviate too far from linear narrative and surface realism.

DH When I started writing for the theatre most of the plays were realist—grotesque realism, or black comedy. I was interested in the poetic and the symbolic. Australian audiences and theatre companies were nervous. In my plays there were no curtains, there were songs, people suddenly doing strange things. I love writing plays with lots of parts. It upset them. And they were nervous about my depictions of women on stage. The role of the female characters in most plays seemed to be to feed lines to the witty male leads.

I've been criticised sometimes for my female characters. I am a feminist and I've always been aware of the lack of three dimensional, lively, gutsy women on stage. Theatre companies are very conservative, they depend on the box office.

MW What about audiences?

DH The question was, would they all boo or would they stay there? People would walk out of my plays in droves. Critics found them confronting or just plain awful, and that didn't help the box office. I had a very chequered career box office wise. In the 70s they would accept a bit more stylistic diversity but the companies were still very conservative.

But I always had support from actors, and from a number of directors whom I'll love till my dying day.

The role of the woman playwright in Australia is incredibly difficult, confronting and disappointing. You had to be really tough to hang in there—really 'stuffed', I nearly said. Maybe that's true too! But if you're really fascinated by theatre, as I am, you keep coming back for more. They can't kick you in the teeth often enough. I wouldn't have missed any of it. And I'm still learning. I feel lucky to have been part of that 1968 generation. I used to say all I needed was a face lift and a sex change.

> *Sue Ingleton (yelling from the audience)*
> *"If you had the sex change Dorothy, you wouldn't need the facelift!"*

DH Our generation thought we'd set up a new indigenous theatre. This was not perhaps something that could last, although we all hoped it would.

MW In your interview with my students, you spoke of being a girl from the bush and really very shy.

DH I still am.

MW Have you developed a persona to protect you from some of the exposure theatre has brought you?

DH The persona is tougher than I really am. I'm just as easily squashed. The person which the media created was a dragon which at times would turn round and bite me. Entrusting my ideas to the media, I'd end up being presented as 'soft in the head' or a 'varicosed Barbie doll'.

> *Dorothy Hewett quotes TS Eliot to illustrate what is required of a writer:*
> *"A condition of complete simplicity, costing no less than everything."*

DH I have learned not to be so vulnerable, to hold back a bit on my private life, not on the page, but in public.

MW You've said it's hard to think of one of your female characters who hasn't ended up disappointed. What does that suggest?

DH I suppose it suggests I am.

It's still difficult for women to be happy, satisfied, to achieve what they set out to achieve. I still think the barriers are there. You've got to be tough and a brave human being to keep challenging those problems. Women do. They keep coming on, again and again, coming back for more.

When your whole life has been given to something, in my case writing and the Communist Party, and the Communist Party goes down the drain, and you wanted to be a great Australian playwright and have your work performed regularly and it isn't, maybe you could be forgiven for having a slightly sardonic view.

MW Helen Keyssar, using Gertrude Stein's term, says a feature of women's play writing is 'landscape'. You've talked about the process of writing a play for you, starting with a 'landscape'.

DH Place is very important. I have to see the set first in my head. Sometimes I have to draw it. When I've got that place right the characters start coming in from the wings and saying things. I'm rather fond of narrators, whether straight out or hidden ones, because the narrator is the link across from the audience to the play.

I've been accused of writing melodramas. I hate well made plays. I loathe and detest them with a bitter hatred. I hate realism almost as much. In my plays I think there's always something happening. I mean, the characters are not just standing there crapping on. I'm always writing three endings. I'm always wanting to go and say something deeper.

I'm very keen on using music. Music is a way of structuring a play. It will lead you on and on. All those little scenes, clunk, clunk. Music is a bridge. It will lead you in a circle.

MW You once said that you think Australians are frightened of the imagination. Do you still think so?

DH I think Australians are very pragmatic people—their life, their history made them so. But you can't say that now, there's such a mix of people here, it's begun to change —not only the way we eat, but the way we think, our imaginations. There's a whole new sensibility happening out there.

MW Are they more frightened of imagination in women?

DH Women's imagination is wild. They're articulating things which have not been articulated in our society. It's brave, it's fresh and it cuts to the bone. It's not afraid, it doesn't pussyfoot around. Women have always been articulate and imaginative.

MW What about the practicalities, how far have you been in on the staging of your plays?

DH When I started, playwrights were either dead or in another country. I was banished from rehearsals. I sat behind the piano till the director spotted me and said "Get her out, I can't stand those blue eyes staring at me!" When I went back I couldn't recognise my play. Standard practice was that the theatre company said, "We don't want to see you until the last two weeks, then you can do the publicity". I began to make certain I was at rehearsals, especially at the beginning and at the end.

*Dorothy told the story of one rehearsal where
she had talked with two of the actors because they had asked her about the play.
The next day the director asked her to leave because she was interfering with his direction.
On the other hand, Rodney Fisher demanded she be at rehearsals.*

MW What advice do you have for an up and coming playwright on how to relate to the rehearsal and directorial processes?

DH If the relationship between the director and writer is marred, the play won't work.

I loathe group devised theatre. That doesn't mean theatre isn't a collaborative process. You've got to be prepared to change it if it doesn't work. But someone is there pulling it all together, using their skills. Their role is absolutely essential. I find it denigrating to a profession to which I've given all my skills, all my time, trying to get better at it, to be told that playwrights should not exist and that the work of the playwright has gone forever. I find this insulting.

I usually re-write everything at least three times, sometimes five, and then again in rehearsal.

MW You've talked about the element of confrontation in theatre—how exposed it is to write for theatre. Adrienne Kennedy calls it a 'bullring' and says women are not happy, or trained to take on the battle it involves. Do you see this as inherent in theatre, or is it to do with structures of theatre as they are now?

DH Women flourish in a supportive environment. Or else you use up so much creative energy hanging in there. When there's a group of people working to create something as well as they can, with respect for one another, it's wonderful.

I don't think it has to be a blood sport, and often it is, and I think that puts women off it puts anybody off, but I think women especially.

MW What are you writing about in your new trilogy?

DH Same old bloody things. Writers tend to repeat themselves. They come at it from different angles. You're trying to create that perfect thing from inside yourself, and you never do, except for two days after you finish a script. You think, I've done it. Then you look at it, and realise you haven't.

Dorothy is writing three plays set in a country town.

MW In the past, you have been criticized by some feminists who've seen your portrayals of women as not particularly positive.

DH You're trying to create on the stage a kind of imaginative, extremely fluid, open ended world in which there is a central female character who is articulate and courageous and in there. It doesn't interest me much whether she wins or loses. What matters is that she is trying to get what she wants. The people in my plays are often marginalised in some ways. The Blue Mountains, where I now live, are full of superannuated hippies, the last of the folkies droning on with his squeeze box, single mothers, pensioners, old women, the unemployed and what I call the 'artisticals' walking up and down the street. The people who don't fit in, don't say the right things. The people who in one way or another are not allowed to speak.

A QUESTION FROM THE AUDIENCE

Q Haven't you and other women playwrights said it all? What's left for young writers to say?

DH There are always things to talk about, the world changes, you've got to have people to interpret it. When I started to write there were things that weren't even touched. The world is born anew all the time, and you're born with it, and you have to experience it and write about it.

MW As PLAYWORKS patron, what advice do you have for younger women writers?

DH Hang in there, kid!

TIMEKEEPER MARION POTTS PEELS ARTICHOKES, PLACES THEM IN A JAR

TES LYSSIOTIS CAN'T MAKE IT TO THE FESTIVAL
BUT SENDS HER PAPER TO BE READ BY EVDOKIA KATAHANAS,
AN ACTOR WHO HAS PERFORMED IN MANY OF HER PLAYS.

His mother has approved of his decision. It is a family matter and the family is going to benefit.
But she hates the abroad where she is going,
and when it comes to his walking out of the house,
she remembers how he was born.

John Berger, *Seventh Man*

Andrea Aloise

the journey

tes lyssiotis read by evdokia katahanas

Two journeys. The first from Greece to Australia. Forty days.
Courage in their hearts, suitcases and glory boxes in their hands.
Forty nights.
Doubts.
Pressed suits in their suitcases.
The first steps into a new country.

We were cleansed of the smells of our homeland. They took us to huge washrooms, damp and misty, and the first ritual of subordination to a new culture began.

We had to show them the palms of our hands, our muscles, and our teeth.
They took blood and urine samples; x-rays.

Australia wanted manual labourers.
So, I came to Australia as a domestic. My husband was classified as a labourer.

Your Introduction to Australia.
Department of Information, October 1948.

The Australians and You.

And now a few words about the Australian themselves.

Perhaps the most important thing is to learn to speak the language of the Australian. Australians are not used to hearing foreign languages. Also try to avoid using your hands when speaking because if you do this you will be conspicuous. There are many other little things you will notice if you watch carefully, for instance, Australian men never wear hair nets. They regard men who do so as effeminate. Australians have a sense of humour that you might find hard to understand at first. They seldom show much enthusiasm about anything. Instead of saying something is magnificent or marvellous, they are more likely to say it is "not bad". And they are very fond of what they call "kidding".

Hotel Bonegilla, 1983.

From World War 2 Europe to Victoria—that's *Hotel Bonegilla*.
From Kythera to the Wimmera—that's *I'll go to Australia and wear a hat*, 1982.

From a stony island to the left of Crete to a cafe in a small
town—that's *The Forty Lounge Cafe, 1990*.

From Firebrace Street, Horsham to Melbourne.
From wheat silos and bull dust to the Big Smoke.

You know what you say when you meet someone you're happy to see, Eleftheria.
Hello nice day.

Sonia   Hello. My glad is very big.

Eleftheria We could have married someone from home. I'm cold.
            You'd better pray for us, you're the priest's daughter.

Sonia   I am. I am. Tí nomízeiw kánv (What do you think I'm doing?)

Eleftheria How did you go on your honeymoon? Vaselli says I'm too noisy.

Sonia   Theo, four times, and he washes after every time and makes me do
            the same.

Eleftheria I was sore at first, maybe he doesn't know how to put in properly. It's big.

Sonia   Big.

Eleftheria Very big.

Sonia   How big?

Eleftheria Mine's big.

Sonia   That big.

Eleftheria That big.

Sonia   A man has to vent his frustrations somewhere.

Eleftheria But he's got a good heart. You can always tell a good man by the eyes.

Sonia   Like a fish.

Eleftheria What have we done, Sonia marrying these old men? You know how many
            young men asked for me in Sydney?

Sonia   He always has an erection. You wouldn't believe it, Eleftheria.
            He wakes up with it every morning. At night it's the same.

Eleftheria The husband is always more greedy for it.

Sonia   I lie there, close my eyes and count the panels in the ceiling and try to
            think of other things. I am naked in our village square. They're all in
            church, I hear my father's voice, there is a greedy rooster with the eyes of
            a fox. He picks at my nipples, my neck. I open my eyes, he stops. I close
            them, he pecks again, plucking a hunk of skin from my neck.

The Forty Lounge Cafe, 1990.

The second journey ...

I've got news for you. Judith, Jennifer, Margaret and me are going to see Spartacus at the matinee. This will be the third time I've seen it, once with Dad and twice by myself. I love the bit when they capture Spartacus and his men, and the Greek—Tony Curtis.

The Romans say "Which one of you is Spartacus?"

Kirk Douglas stands up and says "I'm Spartacus". Then Tony Curtis gets up and says "No, I'm Spartacus". Then this tall negro gets up and says "No, I'm Spartacus". "No, I'm Spartacus. No, I'm Spartacus, No, I'm Spartacus, I'm Spartacus", till the Romans don't know what's going on. I've got news for you.

The Forty Lounge Cafe.

The second journey. An after-image of the first, my own journey as a writer.

From the collective where discussion, the workshop and the group voice was the thing, to nearly having the confidence to call myself a writer.

From teaching drama in state secondary schools to the nurturing arms of La Mama.

From writer/producer/stage-manager/researcher/director cum actor/publicist/sound technician/designer, to having the courage to call myself a writer.

From Bertolt Brecht, John Berger, Joan Littlewood, Pina Bausch, Peter Brook, Garcia Lorca, Theo Angelopoulos, Lina Wertmuller, Isabel Allende, Brothers Taviani, Maria Faradouri, Sylvia Plath, Oriana Fallaci *to* Fallaci, Plath, Faradouri, Taviani, Allende, Wertmuller, Angelopoulos, Lorca, Brook, Bausch, Littlewood, Berger and back to Brecht.

From agit prop to psychological drama.
From historical narrative to intimate, personal vision.

Anna: These little hands. (GRABS THEM, RUBS THEM AGAINST HER FACE). These soft little white hands that soothed me when I had bad dreams. How white your skin used to be—my skin is like an armadillo. Did you think you'd get to heaven easier by suffering? I guess that's the way of saints. I don't believe in heaven or hell, it's all imagination. But we do come from a long line of sufferers, and mother was the best. We Greeks are obsessed by tragedy, love, pain, death. We love a good death.

LAUGHS.

I forgot. In this family we don't talk about bad things, in fact we don't talk at all. It's a dark secret we take to the grave—save it for the journey to the other side, in the glory box.

Then buried deep in the ground we can whisper it to the worms—Mon Dieu, she even kept our baby hair. Packing these plates away Marina?

Each of us has a box—labelled—

*Of course, everything gets put away for later, for the after life—after marriage—after death.
I believe in using things now, they're no good to you dead. Dead is dead.*

*We Papageorge women must prepare for our journey to the other side, the other life
buried deep, deep in our tablecloths, sheets, rugs; smothered in our underwear,
silverware and doilies.*

Blood Moon, 1993.

From seeing plays as being exclusively the domain of English to putting my faith in
bi-lingual, multi-lingual theatre.

03:10 PM

interruption

*ANDREA ALOISE FALLS ONTO THE STAGE IN A POOL OF LIGHT
TO THE LEFT OF EVDOKIA SITTING AT THE TABLE.
EVDOKIA STOPS READING AND LOOKS UP.*

MALA, NEGRA Y FEA
Andrea Aloise

*SHE ENTERS. MUSIC FIT FOR A CIRCUS. DIVES INTO A POOL OF LIGHT AS MUSIC PEAKS. OR
MAYBE SHE HAS JUST BEEN THROWN OUT OF THE LAST PLACE. SHE NOW STRUGGLES WITH
THE DRESS SHE SAW HER MOTHER WEARING TO SOME PARTY LONG AGO. LIKE SOME FISH
SPLATTERING AND FLAILING. IT WANTS TO SUFFOCATE HER, KEEP HER LOW TO THE GROUND,
RESTRAINED. FINALLY, SHE, NOT THE DRESS, WINS. GATHERING HERSELF SHE BEGINS TO DRIFT
UP, UP, UP ONTO HER STILETTOS UNTIL SHE IS FLOATING, DRESS BILLOWING LOOKING AT THE
WORLD BELOW. SHE HAS BROUGHT SOME SUSTENANCE IN THE FORM OF A QUARTERED
ORANGE STUFFED NEATLY INTO HER MOUTH. SLOWLY REMOVING THE FRUIT SHE SAYS:*

I look at you. At your face. I have had that face in my head, hating it. But now that you're
here, it's nothing. You blink, you have your mark, you look at me through your eyes, but
you don't know me, you don't understand, you don't know that you are right not to
understand.

*THE CIRCUS MUSIC BLASTS AGAIN, THROWING HER, PUSHING HER, BULLYING HER.
SHE FINDS SAFETY PUSHED UP AGAINST A WALL. DISORIENTED AND THROWN OFF-BALANCE
SHE PROCLAIMS HER PLIGHT, THE DIFFICULTY OF TAKING A STEP FORWARD.*

I'm standing on a threshold about to enter a room. It is a difficult business. In the first instance I must shove against an atmosphere pressing with a force of fourteen pounds on every square inch of my body. I must make sure of landing on a plank of wood travelling twenty miles per second around the sun. A fraction of a second too early or too late and the plank will be miles away. I must do this while clinging to a round planet hurtling off into space with a wind of ether blowing at God knows how many knots per second, through every interstice of my body.

DEFEATED SHE STAMMERS:

I can't move. I can't move.

MUSIC BY BERNARD HERMANN
TEXT BY DR EDDINGTON

ANDREA LEAVES THE STAGE.
LIGHT UP ON EVDOKIA AT THE TABLE, BACK TO THE JOURNEYS OF TES LYSSIOTIS.

My family's history has pointed me towards an area which I have made my own. The boundaries of this claim were probably pre-determined, but nonetheless, I had to find the X that marked the spot.

Once I started to understand my history, under my mother's guidance, I found the strength to begin scratching the surface. I don't believe that my journey as a writer over the last ten years has led me to new and exotic locations—I haven't taken on "causes". What I have done is persistently mine the one spot—My X.

The first vein I hit gave me everything (the stories of ordinary people) in small quantities, which whetted my appetite for more—so I continue.

Digging in the same spot, I hit other veins which always give me just enough until I hit the next vein. In all of this my journey hasn't been that of a boundary rider but rather of a miner "searching for a heart of gold". Perhaps, the two most telling artefacts I've recovered from my excavation are the suitcase—battered, brown, tied with rope, and the glory box.

For me the suitcase is emblematic of History. If Europe was engulfed in the flood of World War 2 then the suitcase is like the ark sailing to the new land. And if the suitcase is washed on the shores of a lucky country, and if hopes take root there, then the glory box is emblematic of the hopes and dreams of its owners and its owners' children.

The distance between the suitcase and the glory box can't be bridged by a single language—to understand the meaning of each you need both the language of those who carried the suitcases, and the language of those who inherited the glory box.

One year mum decided I should have extra piano instruction. Kalyope was my teacher, she could speak several languages - Arabic, French, Italian, Greek and a bit of English— she enjoyed using a smattering of each throughout the lesson.

Kalyope	Who are these people anyway? They're just barbarians and rabbit farmers.
	I used to be a famous ARTISTE my dear. You know what people used to say to me? You know Kalyope you remind me so much of the great Sarah Bernhardt.
Daughter	And who's Sarah Burntheart? I used to think to myself, some kinda saint or something?
Kalyope	I've toured Alexandria, Beirut, I've been from Paris to Constantinople. In Alexandria, my dear, I played in great theatres with chandeliers, plush seats and perfumes and flowers. I was never a tavern singer, you understand. My dear, I was a famous artiste and wore silk underclothes with real lace. SHE SIGHS DEEPLY.

Her family had sent her out here to help her brother in the shop. One day she was teaching me the French National Anthem. She got so carried away she stood up and sang it, with great passion.

Kalyope	SINGS Allons enfants de la Patrie! La jour de gloire est arrivé! Contre nous de la tyrannie ...

Unexpectedly Mum came in singing the Greek National Anthem.

Mother	Se gnvrízv ap'th kóch Tou spayioú th tromer}
Kalyope	Aux armes, citoyens!
Mother	Ap'ta kókkala bgalména Tvn Ell}nvn ta ierá
Kalyope	Formez vos bataillons!
Mother	Kai sa prQta andrivménh Xaíre, xaíre eleuyeriá
Kalyope	Marchons. Marchons.
Mother	Kai sa prQta andrivménh Xaíre, xaíre eleuyeriá
Daughter	After that I didn't have any more lessons.

To understand you need both Greek and English. The more things change the more they stay the same, the cliché would have it. As with most clichés there's an element of truth, and for me the element of truth is that since I began writing, the bilingual approach has been pivotal to my work.

But does this technique allow lazy opinion makers to always categorise me as "the multicultural woman writer"?

Yep!

From writing/workshopping/writing/workshopping to the splendid isolation of a study, night feeding, a desk—dreaming my work, draft after draft, night and day became one; word by word—in a trance—this was the time I could have been a contender for membership of André Breton's circle in Paris in the 1920s.

In my study still.

In his poem *Ithika* Cavafy says:

Setting out on the voyage to Ithika
you must pray that the way be long......

you must always have Ithika in your mind,
arrival there is your pre-destination.
But do not hurry the journey at all.
Better that it should last many years......

Without Ithika you would not have set out......

Poor though you find it, Ithika has not cheated you
wise as you have become, with all your experience,
you will have understood the meaning of an Ithika.

These lines point to how I'd like to see my own journey as a writer—a single source with many tributaries.

Cavafy's *Ithika* becomes my equivalent of personal history, And my Ithika is full of tales of ordinary madness—more than enough for me.

Excerpts from Tes Lyssiotis' scripts.
reprinted with permission from Currency Press.

saturday

3:55 PM

14:10:1995

ANOTHER ARTICHOKE HEART SLIDES INTO THE JAR.

eat the table

noëlle janaczewska

I'm going to read rather than talk. A piece which not only reflects some of the difficulties I had writing this particular presentation but which also I hope, says something more generally about my writing processes which tend to be eclectic and meandering. The presentation includes extracts from works I've written or am in the process of writing. Some of these extracts are intended to be sung. I'll be reading them however because to my great regret I'm not a good vocalist. Perhaps that's why I write: seeking the transcendental in the musicality of language?

Reflect, Playworks, said on your last ten years as a writer for theatre. In any way you want to. Be innovative! Performative! Immediately I'm anxious, slightly suspicious even, feel a pressure to be funny, entertaining, tell witty anecdotes, and I can't think of a single one. Or is this an attempt to propel me into a writer-performer role? A location I'm not interested in visiting—even on a day trip. After all, it's taken me a long time and a number of wrong turnings into avenues of direction, administration, art theory to be able to focus exclusively on writing—albeit writing not only for performance but also for radio and print, visual art and multi-media contexts, fiction, non-fiction, and most interesting of all to me personally, mixes of the two—fiction and non-fiction. And this focus on my individual biography is also unsettling; resisting autobiography—or more specifically the autobiography of difference—is a current preoccupation. I resent assumptions that every Polish-Australian voice I create is an echo of my own; that the circumstances of every non-Anglo Australian family I describe are those of my own family. Yet, I accept that the forms of biography and autobiography are often important genres in the mapping of post-colonial landscapes in that they allow different voices to speak, and I would not want to deny the facts, the raw material of experience. As Jeanette Winterson says in *Art Objects*[1]:

How each artist learns to translate autobiography into art is a problem that each artist solves for themselves. When solved, unpicking is impossible, we cannot work backwards from the finished text into its raw material ... forcing the work back into autobiography is a way of trying to contain it.

So, resisting the autobiography of difference and the writer-performer model, I head for other destinations; theoretical and abstract ideas, metaphors. I fix on surrealism, back flip further to anthropology—my original training and spend days, weeks, pondering, sketching the possibilities of a surrealist ethnography when I should be writing this presentation. I get caught up in the surrealist gendering of spaces, in questions of the demonic feminine. I re-read one of my favourite books: James Clifford's *The Predicament of Culture*, a work I admire for its inter-disciplinary focus, its adroit negotiation across the compass of ethnography, art and literature. But the Playworks deadline is approaching; where exactly are all these detours taking me? Am I seeking an allegorical mirror, an intersection, a scenic route through this personal history?

57

Wandering ever further away from the subject I'm supposed to be discussing, I revisit favourite sites: the collages of the German Dada artist Hannah Hoch, the marine navigations of Joseph Conrad, the theatrical explorations of Tadeusz Kantor. The linguistic and culinary experiments of Gertrude Stein and Alice B. Toklas: language as reality not representation, an emphasis on rhythm and the incantatory qualities of words, the blurred borders between poetry, prose and performance, writing and cooking. Is this the symmetry I've been seeking? I'm interested in the performative in prose, in the whole menu of possibilities of written text in theatre, the domestic in the philosophical and the semiotic in the kitchen. As well as writing for theatre, I'm also working on a collection of prose pieces: *The Cartographers' Feast*—fiction-essay mixes exploring themes of food and culture in a post-colonial world. Here's an extract from a piece called *Saltfish with Saffron*:

There are wide, wide women in printed skirts,

Punjabi daughters made up to flirt,
Kohl-lined eyes
Beneath grey, Brit. skies,
Piles of limes,
Steel-pan rhymes,
Crates of callaloo and creamy yams
And ganja for sale by the kilogram—
If you're in the know;
Know where to go.
There are adventists and activists
For Jesus, Jah Rastafari and animal rights.
From Jamaica, Jaipur and the local Jubilee estate,
All a-rapping and a-snapping and a-stating their case.
There are old, nut-brown men,
Hallelujah! Amen!
Lifting their feet
To the Trenchtown beat,
And up by The Land of Hope and Glory,
The rhythms of Urdu and Turkish
Spill into the mix
Of stalls of ackee and plantain and salted fish.

On the other side of London, west from the curries and calypso lilt of Ridley Road Market, Saffron and I order dishes of ackee and saltfish, with rice n' peas and baked breadfruit in a tiny cafe crouched under a six lane fly-over in another dull and damp London suburb revitalised by the cultures and cadences of the Caribbean. Winter Fridays, when it's already dark by five o'clock, we lock the door of the Women In Entertainment office where we're both working, and head for this corner of West Indian life and a glass or two of red wine. And to music sweet as gingerbread and as full of promise as a bunch of green bananas, we plot the future stages of our theatrical careers. Saffron is a director and I'm directing my energies into writing, but we're both biding our time in Ladbroke Grove, compiling newsletters, co-ordinating workshops and campaigning for more and better opportunities for women in the arts.

That's a fictional me in London in1985, a few months before I came to Australia. Do we want a bigger slice of the cake, or do we want to bake a whole new one? Arts admin. and The All Ladies No.1 Brush team—a group of women artists based in Amsterdam and London and working across media. We'd just completed our third and fourth works: in the pools and fountains of London's Barbican Centre where we got hauled off by the police and at the Rio Cinema in Dalston where we were offered five minutes of screen time, fee: curry and chips.

And I could go back further: beginning my first theatre company with a thousand pounds and a year's supply of Nivea (we won a magazine competition, sponsored by Nivea, for Women With Vision—or something like that). Or back still further: a primary school nativity play. Passed over for both the Virgin Mary and the Angel Gabriel to end up the back end of the donkey. Or the second parasite in *The Insect Play* when I was about seven. Hardly plum roles.

The Insect Play by the Czech writers Karel and Josef Capek was first performed in Prague in 1922. Influenced by ballet, silent cinema and philosophy, it remains one of my favourite dramas. It uses the insect world as a metaphor for the human condition. I like metaphors, the dreamwork of language, the two-way traffic that criss-crosses the borderlines of the real and the imaginary. The shoreline separating earth and water, the horizon where land and sea ends and the sky begins—spaces of metaphor.

SLIDES FROM Crossing The Water.

Water was the predominant metaphor in my writing up to 1992. Both *Crossing The Water* which I wrote in 1988 and *Shoreline* in 1989 took the Indochinese novels of the French writer Marguerite Duras as their points of departure.

In *Crossing The Water* I used water as a referent for the female body and female sensuality.

SLIDES: Shoreline.

In *Shoreline,* water was a conduit for narrative and inter-textual explorations. *Crossing The Water* was adapted for radio the same year, 1989, and by then it was time to leave Duras, the Saigon harbour-side and the colonial projections of Indochina. Time to reflect waters closer to home.

SLIDES: Black Lagoon.

I wrote *Black Lagoon* in1990 for drama students at Murdoch University in Perth. Influenced by the 1950s science fiction film *The Creature From the Black Lagoon*, notions of scientific knowledge and the history of the atomic bomb, water featured as a site of primal anxiety.

SLIDES: The History Of Water.

The History Of Water was written between 1991 and '92, and first produced in June 1992 by the Sydney Theatre Company's New Stages program. The play explores the space between learning a new language and living in a new language; the difference between floating on the surface of a culture and being able to chart its depths. While I neither see, nor would wish to describe my writing career as an onwards and upwards progression, I do nevertheless see *The History Of Water* as a—sorry about the pun— watershed. Written in English with some Vietnamese, it constituted a shift into new themes different forms and styles; an interest in the theatrical possibilities of writing in more than one language.

The History Of Water received what could at best be termed "mixed" reviews in Sydney, and for a while it seemed as if that was it. I revised the play in the light of what I'd learnt from the season, then put it away. I began work on commissions for community and theatre-in-education plays and on another script of my own initiation: *Cold Harvest*. Wrote short fictions and essays for print. Got a part-time lecturing job at the University of NSW.

Food, theatre and the feminine are frequently conjoined. Why does so much women's writing for theatre and performance end up in seasons of "raw works", in programs of shorts, entrees, appetisers, theatre-in-the-raw? Is our work seen as indigestible, half-baked, unsuitable main course fare? This food-feminine connection intrigues me, offers yet another digression from the task at hand, and before I know it I've ricocheted into Julia Kristeva and notions of the abject. Freud and the uncanny. I'm considering a quick dip into Levi-Strauss's *The Raw and The Cooked*, about to begin to re-read my anthropological motherland—or is it fatherland? (Where is the mother in the fatherland?)—when I realise that time is running out. These digressions must stop—for a while at least. So I swerve back to EAT THE TABLE.

VIDEO: Blood Orange.

Food and the feminine often find their theatrical synthesis through the channels, the issues of body image or eating-behaviour disorders. I explored some of these themes in the work you've just seen—*Blood Orange,* a theatre-in-education play commissioned by Death Defying Theatre in 1992 and 1993. Food, its role in family relationships, its surrounding rituals and folklore replace water as the over-arching metaphor. In *Blood Orange* rhythms and wordplays are foregrounded and become more overtly musical— an essential ingredient and one developed further in a second, 1995 theatre-in-education commission for Death Defying Theatre: *Yungaburra Rd.* This play which used a story-telling format to investigate issues of violence, was influenced by some forms of Asian theatre (Peking Opera and Vietnamese classical, folk and cai luong forms, in particular) and by the melodies and contexts of Portuguese fado. In *Yungaburra Rd.* I tried to blend the spoken and the sung, the poetic and prosaic. The play is set in a Portuguese cafe in Sydney's western suburbs and the audience sit around tables; are part of the world of the Cafe Mundo.

VIDEO: Yungaburra Rd.

Yungaburra Rd., two distinct versions of *Blood Orange* and *The Marie Curie Chat Show*: plays for community theatre and young audiences. In *The Marie Curie Chat Show*, an in-theatre play about women and science I wrote for Salamanca Theatre Company in Hobart, I returned to some of the ideas about the scientific imaginary, technology as symptom and dream that I began to map in *Black Lagoon*.

Marie Curie	*From night dreams to day dreams. From meandering possibilities to meticulously collated thoughts. From mind to matter. Violet Rivers closes her eyes and imagines Olearia Rosa flora. Having conceived of its possibility, she works for its reality; shuffling questions; arranging and rearranging them into different configurations of choice. Faced with the possibility of a new daisy, The Botanist doesn't think a direct solution, but traces instead lines of continuity and probability. Mapping options late into the night while her daughter sleeps.*
Violet Rivers	*Aunty Gwen gives me trees to climb and my very own plot of garden. And then I plant raspberry canes.*
Aunty G/Violet R	*Rubus idaeus.*
Aunty Gwen	*Wallflowers?*
Violet Rivers	*Cheiranthus cheiri.*
Aunty Gwen	*Night-scented stocks?*
Violet Rivers	*Matthiola bicomis—which I germinate from seeds. Why are flowers hardly ever green?*
Marie Curie	*The Botanist thinks her way across maps; poring over soil types, drainage patterns and seemingly unconnected facts and stories.*
Aunty Gwen	*Light falls from the night sky in cascades of silence and immobility. All around the house.*
Violet Rivers	*For my eleventh birthday Aunty Gwen gave me a chemistry set and a lilac tree (Syringa) with deep blue-purple flowers.*

Aunty Gwen	To match the colour of your name.
Violet Rivers	Aunty Gwen was ideas, late nights, bacon sandwiches in front of the TV and rain falling all around the house. Familiar as enamel bowls and water pouring into them while I pored over questions and homework. Aunty Gwen knitted winter sweaters while I tried to knit together the pieces of my world. She was warm as tea and forthright as film. (PAUSE.) Every girl needs an Aunty Gwen.

From *The Marie Curie Chat Show*, 1994

Community and theatre-in-education, although a part of my writing, are contexts that are not without their limitations, and I'm aware that women writers especially can get fenced into these squares on the theatrical grid.

I began researching *Cold Harvest* in 1993 with a Literature Board fellowship. The opportunity to create a piece without either the time or content constraints of a commission. In this play I wanted to explore metaphors of the cold, of shopping, migration and food in less literal and more symbolic ways, and I wanted to try generating a work in two languages rather than writing in English and relying on translation. Most of my Polish vocabulary centres on food and family relationships. I considered updating my Polish, but decided instead to let my very unequal knowledge of the two languages shape the text. And a trip to one of the last Cold War frontiers between North and South Korea added another geography, another war, another language to *Cold Harvest*:

Kasia	The Korean tour guide points out glass-fronted booths where interpreters sit and translate war into a kind of uneasy peace.
Mi-Kyoung	(SINGING) As we look across This in-between— Neither north nor south, East nor west—I see a flock of Manchurian cranes Swell up from the snow, And I watch them as they fly Back and forth: North to south South to north.
Kasia	Over forty years ago 'The Bridge of No Return' marked the end of a war. Now it marks the end of a country, an ideology, an 'economic miracle'.
Mi-Kyoung	As we leave, the hills of north Korea, pale blue-grey in the winter light, fade into the distance, and ahead rise the hills of South Korea—looking exactly the same.

Kasia	North
Mi-Kyoung	South
Kasia	The East
Mi-kyoung	We in the West
Kasia	West of what?
Mi-kyoung	West of East
Kasia	Which East?
Mi-kyoung	East
Kasia	The Far East?
Mi-kyoung	The Eastern Bloc?
Kasia	Eastern Europe?
Mi-kyoung	East Asia?
Kasia	We in the West
Mi-kyoung	Who live in the South
Kasia	But if Australia is South—
Mi-kyoung	And West—
Kasia	And South Korea—
Mi-kyoung	Is North
Kasia	And West—
Mi-kyoung	North Korea is North—
Kasia	But East—
Mi-kyoung	Poland is North—used to be East
Kasia	Now moving West
Mi-kyoung	Where is the centre?

From *Cold Harvest* third draft, 1995.

In *Cold Harvest* two contemporary Sydney families, the Kims and the Kozlowskis. A son is getting married. A wedding cake is being made.

As the various family rituals and tensions unfold around this celebration, two daughters interrogate their Korean and Polish traditions to ask where they fit into them, and what it means to be Australian in the 1990s. How can they find the answer to that eternal migrant question of how to have your cake and eat it?

Cold Harvest explores differences between first and second generation migrants, and focuses specifically on the dilemmas of second generation migrants caught in the cross-fire between then and now, there and here, 'us' and 'them'. The negotiations they make across cultures, histories and languages as they attempt to understand the Cold

War politics of their parents' generation, attempt to reconcile a polarised past with a culturally diverse present. Through the central figures of Kasia, a second generation Polish-Australian, and Mi-Kyoung, a second generation Korean-Australian, *Cold Harvest* looks at food, tradition, family secrets, mythologies of the homeland, shopping and consumerism, the weather, the Cold War and the things we choose to remember and to forget.

Why are Sally and Tony Kim so upset when Mi-Kyoung pretends to be Japanese? Why do Kasia's parents, Franciszka and Tadeusz, have no photos of their wedding?

What is tradition? Why is it important? Do new rituals and customs evolve, or are they created? What does it mean when cultural rites are co-opted for commercial purposes?

For both Kasia and Mi-Kyoung, a journey to the country of their parents' birth is an important part of their discovery of their Australian identity. For Kasia who is well-versed in Polish history, it's a search for an individual past that has been hidden. For Mi-Kyoung, the situation is the reverse: she knows inside-out her mother's and father's personal stories, but lacks a sense of the broader national history of her parents' homeland. *Cold Harvest* is structured around metaphors of food, shopping and the cold; around an investigation of the migrant dream of a 'better life'. The striving for material security, for educational and professional success and the frictions, anxieties and conflicting desires these produce in a second generation living in the bi-cultural spaces of modern Australia.

Food is an important metaphor in this play. Part of the design consists of a cold store —a glass storehouse stacked with jars of jams, pickled vegetables and conserves; the past literally preserved and sealed. And a wedding cake—surely one of the most symbolic foods of all—is planned and discussed. Helpful hints are exchanged; cooking tips guaranteed to make the icing on the cake as white and smooth as snow.

The play interweaves a number of strands and stories. It integrates music, song, rhythm, puppetry, cooking, a stylised choreography and three languages to capture the sense of linguistic and emotional fragmentation of living in more than one culture.

Questions of tradition and cross-culturalism shape the form as well as the content of the play. Both Korean and Polish cultures have strong and vibrant performance traditions of story-telling, metaphor and poetic drama, and *Cold Harvest* draws on these theatricalities to create a theatre text which integrates traditional and modern myths and rituals into a contemporary Australian setting.

Kasia: Food was used to open conversations, close discussion, change the subject and control information. When I begin to ask questions I'm subjected to a barrage of food, so I feel I'm fighting my way through forests of red cabbage, wading through seas of grainy soup and slicing my way across mountains of cake. It's no co-incidence the only Polish vocabulary I know revolves around food: krupnik (barley soup), zupa jezynowa ze smietanka (blackberry soup with sour cream), nadziiewane ogorki (stuffed cucumbers), makowiec (poppy seed cake), dzem truskawkowy (strawberry jam), konfitura Ciotki Juliany (Aunt Juliana's jam)... I know three different Polish words for jam, but I can't tell someone I love them.

From *Cold Harvest*, third draft, 1995.

Cold Harvest is being developed with the assistance of Playworks.

Last year, 1994, *The History Of Water* begins something of a renaissance with a radio adaptation, awards and overseas productions and publication. I move from the Department of Theatre and Film at the University of NSW to the Department of Media and Text at UTS. Wonder if teaching is as much of a trap for women as cooking?

04:10 PM ━━━━━━━━━━━━ **interruption**

*LIGHTS SUDDENLY COME UP
AND THE LIVE VIDEO CAMERA PICKS UP JANE GOODALL
MAKING VEGEMITE AND PEANUT BUTTER SANDWICHES AT THE DESK.*

SANDWICH

Food is used to open conversations, close discussions, change the subject and control information.

Yes, well. I would like to change the subject. All this talk about food is depressing me. But I can't change the subject. It's got to me. Either cooking or teaching. Some of us only had one of those options. Some of us never had a hope at the other. Some of us were beyond help before multi-cultural Australia started to happen. Some of us were brought up in the outer suburbs of Adelaide in the 1950s, the new clean, sterile suburbs where the most exciting experience of your childhood was sleeping in the front yard on a camp bed on hot nights, while the huntsmen galloped across the lawn underneath. Keith Gallasch (in Open City's *Photoplay* 1988 & 1994) might have passed our place as he vomited up Devonshire tea in the back of his parents' car on the way home from Mount Lofty on Sunday afternoons. Devonshire teas were the cutting edge of Adelaide cuisine.

Either/or. That was what food was about in those days. You could go down to the local shop and buy either pink cake or white cake, either white bread or brown bread, either Neapolitan ice-cream or white ice-cream. You could have your sandwiches with either peanut butter or Vegemite, and your Mum could cut them straight or diagonal, making four triangles or four squares. My Mum never even gave us that choice. There were too many kids and diagonal was too much fuss. She said the triangles were too fiddly to put in the plastic lunchboxes. There was one boy in my class whose sandwiches were different. His Mum made the bread herself and cut big chunks, stuck together with home-made pickle. And she put only one cut in them so he used to sit there with his great fat rectangle, holding it with both hands so he could cram it in his mouth. On week-ends we had lunch at home. Either chops or mince with boiled sprouts. Sometimes my sister and I used to go and hide from lunch.

Either/or. Well, it was teaching or teaching for me, Noëlle. Is that a predicament of culture or what? I guess I could have tried to be an artist, but if autobiography is the raw material of art—and you are what you eat—what could I have done with an autobiography whose formative phase reduces to a trial of blunt cut sandwiches?

So, now I can say, if you can't hack the sandwiches, try the metaphors. A sandwich is a great metaphor, don't you think? Simple, yet multi-purpose. Quick to prepare. No more of this either/or stuff. You be the cook, I'll be the teacher, and we'll stick together. You be the artist, I'll be the anthropologist. And what should come between us? No, I tell you what, you prepare a paper and I'll make it into a sandwich by filling in the middle with this interruption. Call me the jam.

It's not often you get to interrupt a writer or performer. This is a new kind of option for me, to tell you the truth. Well, what do you know. Maybe the options are opening up at last. Usually I just sit here quietly in the dark, being an audience to what you write, to what is performed. Now don't get me wrong. I don't resent that. But I do like the options to be opened up. When I came to see *The History of Water* here at the Sydney Theatre Company a few years ago, the audience was over half Vietnamese and they'd opened up the options quite a bit. They brought their kids with them. Little kids, who roamed about the auditorium, and occasionally went to explore outside it. Parents or grandparents would get up from time to time to corral some stray kid. What I don't like about the theatre is being shut in. Because going out of this enclosure during a live performance is such a heavy statement.

Either/or. When I moved to Sydney in the early 70s you either went to see David Williamson at the Nimrod or Tom Stoppard hosted by the Elizabethan Theatre Trust. Home grown or imported. I didn't know about Inhibodress, I'm ashamed to say. Once I tried to see *Waiting for Godot* but my partner and I were the only people who came so they cancelled it. That is a true story, cross my heart and hope to die.

HER SANDWICH TOPPINGS BECOME MORE VARIED. SHE SCATTERS A VARIETY OF LEAVES, A CAPSICUM, MAYONNAISE, ETC.

The options have opened up in the last ten years—Playworks, The Performance Space, Boomalli, Open City, Artspace—options have been bursting out all over, the edge is cutting in all directions. Keep the lid off the sandwich, go for the 3D topping.

Cooking, teaching, making metaphors, interrupting. Could I do this interrupting thing for a living, do you think? I'd like that. I'll be a predator, feeding off the well-prepared. Who should I interrupt next? I could get ambitious, start thinking big. An archbishop would be good. Or the Minister for the Arts. I could teach him ... You go back to your paper now, Noëlle, while I just cook something up.

Jane Goodall

LIGHTS UP ON NOËLLE JANACZEWSKA WHO TAKES UP HER READING.

Combining explorations of food and multicultural Australia however, enters difficult terrain. As Sneja Gunew says in an essay entitled "Feminism and The Politics of Irreducible Difference", cuisine is an easy and relatively unthreatening way of discussing cultural diversity[2]. A context in which it's as easy to mix as a White Wings chocolate cake. The ethnic restaurant the palatable face of difference. Pictures of happy, dancing, singing, eating extended ethnic families. Rodzina, Dziadek, Babcia, Matka, Coreczka, Sostry, Tatus, Brat, Ciotki ...But why is it that many of these images of multi-cultural Australia often posit conservative notions of family and sexuality? I want to critique these warm and fuzzy, safe and nostalgic notions of multi-cultural Australia.

Historia, another work-in-development scheduled for production in February next year, explores the intersections of ethnic and sexual identities, interweaving two relationships, one contemporary and one historical.

In contemporary Sydney two women, Zosia and Zoe begin an affair. Both are negotiating difficult and dangerous terrain. Zoe is married to Martin, and Zosia is trying to find a way to connect to her Polish heritage without also embracing conservative and restricting notions of family and sexuality.

Zosia and Zoe both grew up in Sydney's outer western suburbs, but have as adults moved away from the landscapes and limitations of their early teenage years in Penrith and Westmead. Connected by desire, electronic mail and a number of more or less clandestine encounters, Zosia and Zoe re-visit the places of their early sexual experiences. Stories and personal histories are revealed and swapped, and through this exchange the intimacy between Zosia and Zoe develops.

The Artist and The Anthropologist, fictional characters I've based very loosely on the historical figures of writer and artist Stanislaw Witkiewicz and anthropologist Bronislaw Malinowski, grew up in turn-of-the-century Krakow in Poland. They were lovers before The Anthropologist left for London to pursue an English career. In 1914

The Anthropologist invited his friend to join him on an ethnographic expedition to Australia. This desert journey pushes their relationship to a point of crisis. The Artist longs for the intimacy they shared in Krakow, but The Anthropologist, seeking academic and social respectability in England, struggles to deny their Polish past.

The two women are also linked by Zosia's interest in the love story of two men: The Artist and The Anthropologist. Zosia sees in their relationship a way to connect to her cultural heritage without denying the complexities of her own sexuality. She works across language and culture to uncover and piece together information about The Artist and The Anthropologist. For Zoe, Zosia's Polish background is romantic and exotic; a stark contrast with what she sees as the cultural poverty of her own adolescence in suburban Sydney. But as Zosia reveals to her lover the facts and fictions, the rumours and speculation about the relationship between the two men, Zoe too becomes drawn into their story. She discovers in it a compelling symmetry: are she and Zosia repeating the same patterns of rapture and denial?

Zoe   *The car turns into Westbury Road. I hear the wet rasp of its tyres*
          shouldering the gravel in front of the house. The beam of its headlights
          sweeps vinyl wood, repeat patterns, empty spaghetti tins and SAO crumbs.
          I flick off the TV and my sister Louise puts on the kettle to make a cup of
          tea for Mum home from work.

          We undress cowboys almost every night. Watched by bears. Teddy bears.
          Me and my sister in our bedroom Mum keeps promising to redecorate,
          but never does with its twin beds and chipboard cupboard that divides my bit
          from Louise's. I'm always on the side of the wallpaper Indians and Louise has
          always got her favourite cowboy. After we turn out the light, she tells me
          about him, what he'd look like if he stripped off his wallpaper clothes.
          But she always stops at his wallpaper belt, and I tell her to go on—go on—but
          she never does. So I promise to do her homework for a week if she can get
          his pants off and she does—she does, but underneath his trousers ... he's
          wearing Speedos—(# LAUGHING. He's got back on his wallpaper horse and
          ridden off into the wallpaper sunset, and anyway, Zo, you're older than me,
          so you must know more about, you know—men's things).

          But the only man's body I've seen naked was Mr. Rogers-from-round-the-
          corner, sitting on the edge of our mother's bed when I wandered in one
          morning to ask for bus fare money and Mum hurried me out and made me
          wait in the kitchen. And after that, Mr. Rogers-from-round-the-corner never
          came back to our house, so all my ideas about men concentrated into those

wallpaper figures. And I'd keep on looking at them, hoping that if I looked hard enough their wallpaper clothes would peel away and I'd see the body beneath.

From *Historia* fourth (rehearsal) draft, 1995.

Wallpaper is one of the predominant metaphors of *Historia*. Papering over the cracks. whitewashing, covering up. Family scenes, florals, repeat patterns and flocks against which the two female characters could easily become invisible.

The narrative structure of *Historia* is deliberately fluid, offering partial and fragmented narratives within a spatial, rather than a time-based, framework. The play's various locations are tangible, intangible and remembered: Penrith, Westmead, Krakow, the Australian desert, present day Sydney, the spaces of memory and the electronic space of the Internet. And although the various locations each give rise to their own specific stories, meanings and resonances, they also overlap and interact. Images, emotions and narrative threads from one space echoed in another.

Both couples push at the boundaries of their environments. The two men question themselves and each other amid the vast expanse of the desert. The two women chip away at backgrounds of insistent domesticity and family obligations.

THE HUM AND BEEP OF ELECTRONIC COMMUNICATION AND VOICES WHISPERING IN DIFFERENT LANGUAGES BLENDS WITH THE MUSIC OF SZYMANOWSKI.

Zosia   *Your words fall down like rain*
             Upon a violet sea.
             Your message superimposed over mine
             Spreads your body across
             The matrix of the screen,
             Across the horizontality of the land;
             And I no longer try
             To understand the language,
             But hear instead the shimmer of colour
             That polishes laughter.

THE LANDSCAPE DARKENS

TWO MEN KISS, THEN PULL APART. CAUGHT IN THE FLICKERING LIGHT OF A PASSING TRAIN.

Zoe	Martin's caught a fish.
Zosia	Just the one?
Zoe	I don't know.
Zosia	I turn off the caress
	Of your electronic tongue;
	Revert to the stretch and flex
	Of the screen wallpaper
	As it flickers fish and stars
	Like flames and sparks
	Across the pixel skin of midnight blue.

DARKNESS

TWO WOMEN KISS. THEY TOO ARE LIT UP BY THE MOVING LIGHTS OF A PASSING TRAIN.

DARKNESS. THE WIND HOWLS. THE PAGES OF THE ABANDONED BOOKS FLUTTER.
THE ONLY LIGHT COMES FROM THE TWO COMPUTER SCREENS.

IT BEGINS TO RAIN.

THE SZYMANOWSKI FADES OUT.

From *Historia*, fourth (rehearsal) draft 1995.

I'm interested in ideas; abstractions and metaphors, narrative exploration and the rhythms, materialities and idiosyncrasies of language. I see language like music, performance forms like composition, and I think that music—in its broadest sense— is becoming more and more important in my work. I'd love to write a musical or a libretto. I'm interested in geographies and plays and performance texts. In a sense of character rather than realistic biographies. I reject the head-heart opposition of intellect and emotion. Ideas can be passionate and the emotions are not without reason and circumspection. Often I work with an associative, poetic kind of logic rather than with the more conventional dramatic logic of character journeys, plot development and conflict. I do not believe that conflict is necessary to make dynamic, enjoyable and challenging theatre. As the Chilean writer and film-maker, Raul Ruiz points out in *Poetics of Cinema*:

To say that a story can only take place if it is connected to a central conflict forces us to eliminate all stories which do not include confrontation and to leave aside all those events which require only indifference or detached curiosity, like a landscape, a distant storm or dinner with friends—unless such scenes punctuate two fights between the bad guys and the good guys. Even more than scenes devoid of any action, central conflict theory banishes what are called mixed scenes: an ordinary meal interrupted by an incomprehensible incident with neither rhyme nor reason, and no future either, so that it all ends up as an ordinary meal once more.[3]

Rules like central conflict theory are not neutral and value free, but serve particular interests and are answerable to specific histories, so I can't countenance the old adage: "learn the rules first then you can break them". It seems to me the moment you posit rules you have created a centre and a periphery; a relationship of authority and opposition, a context in which any work perceived to be "breaking the rules" can be safely shifted to the margin.

That's how I see things, and those are the perspectives, views and enthusiasms I seek to translate into my writing.

1. Winterson, Jeanette. *Art Objects*, (London: Jonathan Cape, 1996), p. 106.

2. Gunew, Sneja. "Feminism and the Politics of Irreducible Differences", in Sneja Gunew & Anna Yeatman (eds.) *Feminism and the Politics of Difference*, (St Leonards: Allen & Unwin, 1993) , p. 16.

3. Ruiz, Raul. *Poetics of Cinema*, Brian Holmes (trans.) (Paris: Editions Dis Voir, n.d.), p. 11.

13   ▷ I3A   14

13   ▷ I3A   14

writing ningali

angela chaplin

*NINGALI LAWFORD'S SOLO PERFORMANCE IN THREE LANGUAGES (NINGALI)
HAS BEEN SEEN IN FREMANTLE, KALGOORLIE, CANBERRA AND MELBOURNE
AND AT THE EDINBURGH FESTIVAL, IN BERLIN AND LONDON.
NINGALI HAS GONE HOME TO BROOME AND CAN'T BE COAXED TO THE CITY
FOR THE FESTIVAL. ANGELA CHAPLIN,
ARTISTIC DIRECTOR OF DECKCHAIR THEATRE IN FREMANTLE
WHO COLLABORATED WITH NINGALI AND ROBYN ARCHER ON THE WORK,
SPEAKS ABOUT THE WRITING PROCESS.*

Ningali Lawford and I had been friends for some time before we began the formal work on the play *Ningali—her story so far*. A couple of years into our friendship, we worked together for the first time when Ningali performed as a dancer-actor-singer in a piece produced by Deckchair Theatre called *My Spiritual Dreaming* by Eddie Bennell which I directed. A large scale piece for the Festival of Perth, *My Spiritual Dreaming* led to a great deal of partying and it was during these social events that I noticed the effect of Ningali's presence and storytelling on other people. She was magnetic, her stories interesting, her presence intriguing. There are not many performers that a director will decide to do a one person show with. The ability to run the marathon on stage, hit the wall and keep going belongs to very few performers—Ningali is one such performer. I started to talk to her about creating a one person show about her life.

A short time later, Robyn Archer saw Ningali in *My Spiritual Dreaming* and after discussions with us both, came on board the making/writing team. Our primary responsibilities were divided between Ningali performing, me directing and Robyn completing the final text. We were all responsible for making/writing the show.

So, in July 1994, a couple of years after the talking had begun we finally began the formal process of making the show. Four of us took off in a car to drive from Fremantle to Fitzroy Crossing in the Great Sandy Desert of North-West Australia—the equivalent of four full days driving. I put a microphone in front of Ningali in the car and started asking questions beginning with, "Ningali, what's the first thing you remember in your life?". Gradually we began to build a body of background research and storytelling material.

During the next two weeks we visited Ningali's community and spent some time with her family, then travelled back to Broome where Ningali and I spent a week alone creating a rough shape for the show and deciding on the stories, the order of material, writing new pieces and determining which pieces would be in which of the three languages, English, Kriol and Walmajarri.

At this point, Robyn Archer flew into Broome and we headed back to Wangkatjungka, Ningali's community. Robyn saw her first run-through of our material in the backyard of the Fitzroy Crossing Backpackers. From there, listening to the tapes, using our rough shape for the show and asking more questions, she started to write a first draft.

Back in Broome we spent a night at Cable Beach relaxing, left Robyn to complete a final draft and started on the long journey back to Fremantle. More interviews, more taping and more discussions took place on the three days drive home.

Once back in Fremantle, rehearsals continued—a few days later, Robyn flew in with a draft that incorporated all of the work that we had done to date along with some new material she'd added plus the deft language of an "actual" writer. Draft two came in the last week of rehearsal and further cuts and pastings happened after the first preview.

Opening night worked extremely well and the success of the piece is, as they say, history.

From the moment we got into that car in Fremantle to head north until opening night was a period of five weeks. The process was only possible in that time because we lived and breathed the project for that entire period, also because we shared a sense of humour and we both liked a cold beer in the shade of a tree in a very beautiful part of Australia.

TRIBAL SONG—SAD AND ANXIOUS
SPEAKING IN KRIOL SHE DRAMATISES A CONVERSATION.

But what about these dreaming sites
What about the river?
How are we going to do law properly if we can't
tread on our own land?
We know station work—highly skilled
Suddenly put down to the lowest
Biggest mob ever. Never seen so many
Nothing to do—the one thing they can do
they're not allowed to do any more.
Fences—can't hunt goanna
Can't go to the Fitzroy River—what about the fish?
What about the frogs for diet in sad time?
How we gunna teach kids to hunt
when we can't go anywhere?

Proper big loss, nowhere to go, no work to do,
no pride to have—just pension and God, or grog
That's the two ways it was—two extremes—
either real religious—or proper big sinner
Great Depression—but this one didn't have any finish line
Just had fences—and sitdown money.

SHE PICKS UP A CAN OF BEER, GOES TO THE MICROPHONE AND
STARTS STAND-UP ROUTINE.

I tell ya what,
Like, the worse it gets the funnier it is.
There was this old couple at Fitzroy Crossing and they got arrested for drunk
and disorderly and fighting on the access road to the Inn. They turned up next day
in the Magistrate's Court—the old man was being charged, and the old lady,
sitting there still with matted hair from where he'd hit her over the head with a stick.
The magistrate looks at him real serious and asks:
'What do you plead?'
Suddenly the old girl jumps up
'I the one who pleed—look ere, pleed all in me 'ead'.
'Was it in self-defence?' asks the magistrate.
Up jumps the old girl again.
'I'm the one, who make me jump the ploody fence!'

In the end, the magistrate says
'Well, there are many things to consider before I make my judgement. I want to ask you,
do you have any previous record?'
'Record?' says the old man, 'Big mob record! Got Slim Dusty, Jim Reeves, Buddy Williams.
Yeah, real big mob record'

SHE SPEAKS IN KRIOL.

... I couldn't work out how they put such a rude song
on the radio, and singing it everywhere.
See we got this word 'budya' means kind of female genitalia,
So I'm listening to cunt-ry music all the time and I hear:
(SINGS) "Budya sweet lips a little closer to the phone ..."
Well, I've heard of telephone sex but that's just ...
Thank you, thank you ...
(SINGS) Budya sweet lips a little closer

SHE SPEAKS IN WAMBAJARRI TO EXPLAIN THE JOKE.

Suddenly I left Fitzroy, my love, my family again. I was in Sydney at the Aboriginal and Islander Dance Theatre.

SHE GOES INTO A STRICT AND STRENUOUS CONTEMPORARY DANCE ROUTINE, SWEATING OUT A MONOLOGUE AT THE SAME TIME.

We did tap, we did traditional
We did dance from all over the place
We did jazz, we did Method
We did movement, we worked up the pace
I'd always known about ballet
known about girls on their toes
Now we started to get Martha Graham
and mixing up cross-cultural impros

We did lifts, we did tribal
We used dancing north, south, east and west
We did pas de deux and solos
And we sure as hell worked up a sweat

My Jabbi and Jajja came to Sydney
They were so funny
Before they came, one of the mob had said
to my old fire-stick (my old flame, you say).

SHE SPEAKS IN KRIOL.

Hey I need that bankbook
What do you need bankbook for? Put money in?
Nuh, don't want that bankbook put money in
Want that bankbook with the photo in—to go to Sydney
He was talking about a passport.

MAYBE NINGALI ADOPTS A BIT MORE TRIBAL POSITION—
AT THE FIRE. IT'S MYSTERIOUS AND SHE SPEAKS IN THAT VOICE HER AUNTIE USED SOMETIMES,
WHISPERING ON THE INTAKE OF BREATH.

... My Jabbi taught our dances at the school
He couldn't work out about rehearsing
he just reckoned we do it,
I'd seen him get up and dance
and thought he's so old—he'll have to give this away

But on the night we performed, I was real proud
the boys were all dressed up in our painting
and our colours
Suddenly Jabbi jumped up out of the audience
from nowhere—and started joining in. He just did it.
I was in the middle of this dance and I started crying,
I was crying for my Jabbi. He joined in and did a big solo

I was very proud of him
I was proud of being from Wankatjunka
and I didn't want to be from anywhere else
I realised, completely now, what he was talking about
I hadn't lost my language
and I was proud of my background ...

From *Ningali,* 1994.

20   **KODAK 5053 TMY**   21   KO

20   **KODAK 5053 TMY**   21   KO

publishing performance

SUZANNE CHAUNDY SPEAKS TO KATHARINE BRISBANE OF CURRENCY PRESS.

Currency Press will be twenty-five years old this year. In that time, we have published the work of some 160 playwrights, of which 60 are women. It's not exactly equitable but it reflects the theatre industry in Australia; and the proportion is a great deal better today than it was ten years ago.

It is the writers themselves that have made the difference. In the 1970s there was pioneering work by the Women's Group at the Pram Factory in Melbourne; and in 1981-82 further consciousness-raising through the Women Directors' Workshop and the Women and Theatre Project at the Nimrod Theatre in Sydney. As with all movements, the early work was polemical and took time to mature. And mature it did. In 1981 only Dorothy Hewett and Alma de Groen held places on the mainstage. Today we have a canon to be proud of, with writers like Hannie Rayson, Katherine Thomson, Jill Shearer, Tes Lyssiotis, Mary Morris, Joanna Murray-Smith, Noëlle Janaczewska, Heather Nimmo, Eva Johnson, Debra Oswald, Tobsha Learner, Hilary Bell and Anna Broinowski. Jennifer Compton is back in the field again. Doreen Clarke, alas, has vanished. The wonderful Betty Roland died this year, aged 92; but Oriel Gray joins our list later this year, aged 78.

What is particularly significant about these writers and others like them is the way they have sought performance—through community theatre, youth theatre, radio, amateur competitions. The joint strength of individuals and the encouragement of the Australia Council have built a climate of confidence from which we have all benefitted. Gender studies have contributed a new market for a female perspective.

For Currency Press the prime criterion in choosing a play is: 'Is it good of its kind?' After that, marketing forces come into play. All the plays by our women authors are very good of their kind and by degrees are demonstrating that there is a genuine female perspective to the creation of drama both in content and form. This year we publish *Three Greek-Australian Plays* by Tes Lyssiotis; Debra Oswald's compelling drama of dysfunctional families, *Gary's House*; *What Is The Matter With Mary Jane?* by Wendy Harmer—the actor Sancia Robinson's story of suffering an eating disorder; Margaret Kirby's dramatic debate on the ordination of women, *My Body, My Blood*; Jenny Kemp's performance work *The Black Sequin Dress*; Mary Morris's stage adaptation of Morris Gleitzmann's *Blabbermouth* and Paige Gibb's adaptation of Tim Winton's *Lockie Leonard Human Torpedo*; and Oriel Gray's *The Torrents*, written in 1955. A *Gay and Lesbian Anthology* will include work by Sandra Shotlander, Eva Johnson, Alison Lyssa and Margaret Fischer.

1 ▷ 1A 2

1 ▷ 1A 2

shorts program

susie bromfield, alison lyssa, sarah brill, anni finsterer
directed by: sally richardson

Ros Horin

Playworks was an idea that came to me after witnessing the whole process of the Women and Arts Festival (1982) in which a number of women writers were given an opportunity for public production for the first time and were really shot down in flames by the critics. There was great expectation around that festival. Suddenly, here were some women artists on stage. And then they were judged up against the really established Australian male writers in quite harsh terms. I felt that the whole process had been a very negative one for a lot of women because expectations had been so raised and it was just a one-off event. I really felt that what was needed was something much more long term and enduring where women writers would have a chance to develop in a more protected, low profile environment before emerging into the public arena. I feel it's very destructive for artists to be thrust out into the public eye before they're ready. I did see a number of careers destroyed by the shock of that exposure.

As a director, I'd found myself drawn to the new English women writers and some from New York and I was looking for these kinds of writers in Australia. I strongly believe that the play's the thing—if you haven't got a good script it doesn't matter how exciting the production is. So I thought, right, we've got to see more images of women on stage. We've got to develop Australian writers and to do it we've got to find a process that is flexible and enduring and is going to give us the depth of development we need. So I called together a group of friends, female artists, mainly directors, and a couple of writers and we brainstormed how we might get this project up and running.

We made significant progress each year. We probably started with processes that were more structured than where we sit currently and they were very much to do with educating writers. In the first year we set up a number of forums and seminars and lectures, trying to look at the difference between writing for theatre and television and film, trying to get writers to understand the acting process and what actors contribute, what designers contribute. So it was initially a process of educating writers at the same time as looking at their embryonic ideas and exploring them. Over the five year period, the process was constantly up for review by all of the committee involved. Gradually it developed into something that was much more tailored to the individual needs of each writer. And I think that's still very much the case today. But each year of those first five, we were able to say at the end of each year here's a play that's been developed by Playworks and it's now having a production. So there were measurable results in terms of product as well as a very stimulating and energetic network of artists that was coming together. At the end of each year when we'd sit down and decide whether to apply for another grant or not we'd go through quite a rigorous process of evaluation. Was there still a need for us to exist or not? Had the parity of women writers increased out there in the Australian theatre environment? And certainly for the five years I was there, we thought there was valid reason to continue. And I think now that even though the situation for Australian women writers has improved in the last ten years, there is still reason to continue.

One of our key philosophical commitments was to developing a flexible process and never getting entrenched—I think that's been one of our strengths. The organisation has now developed in such a way that it's much more committed to the research and development side of writing for performance and to a full exploration of process and I think it's providing an alternative, an investigation that's not happening anywhere else in Australian theatre. That in itself is a valid reason for Playworks to continue.

Virginia Baxter

Playworks offers writers a set of possibilities. It's an organisation that shies away from the idea that there is only one way to write a play: that there is a model and as long as we all have that very clear cut model in our heads, drilled into us and we obey the rules of theatre, we will all write the well-made play. We all know that writing doesn't work that way, that writers work in many different ways and that careers don't necessarily go onward and upward but veer mysteriously from one realm into the other, depending on who you're writing for, for instance, what happens to your writing in the process of collaboration with other people, having your work produced by other people ... What Playworks offers, on the one hand, is a network of support for writers that says, we want to hear what you have to say about your writing, where you think it might be going, details of the performance you might be imagining, the audience you want to speak to; and we'll help you as far as possible to achieve your goals for your work. And along the way, if we can offer you some exciting ideas that you hadn't thought of, even better. We try to be as flexible as we can and to respond to the range of work that comes our way—and we encourage the broadest possible diversity of work to come our way. We've put writers into contact with choreographers, composers, designers. We've offered writers, say, two very different interpretations of a script. One performer-writer wanted to incorporate video into her performance and needed time to work with a video maker. We've provided writers of very spare texts with performance ideas that they can take away and incorporate into new drafts. And that flexibility pays off. We run all kinds of workshops for writers, lots of them to do with writing the body into performance, making plays performative. Writers appreciate the chance to see things in different ways and they make contacts—another really big part of what Playworks does—putting writers into contact with other theatre workers, providing an intellectual and emotional milieu. Working relationships are set up and collaborations spring from those relationships. We also acknowledge that there are a large number of companies in Australia at the moment—youth theatres, community theatres, contemporary performance venues, the new media network— and a growing audience for this work. What comes with that is the possibility of an enormous range of writings. So as well as encouraging mainstage theatres to produce more work by women writers, Playworks aims to encourage women writers to be strongly represented in all spheres of performance writing, rather than desperately seeking to make it into that one very narrow stream called the mainstream.

> From *Playing With Time*, a radio program celebrating Playworks' tenth annivesary, produced for ABC Radio National's *Fictions* program by Sally Richardson and Anne Wynter.

SALLY RICHARDSON ALSO DIRECTED THIS PROGRAM ENTITLED SHORTS *FEATURING EXCERPTS FROM WORK IN DEVELOPMENT IN PLAYWORKS' 1995 PROGRAM. READINGS BY ANNI FINSTERER, ALAN FLOWER, WENDY STREHLOW AND JUDY FARR ARE "INTERRUPTED" BY THE RECORDED VOICES OF THE FOUR WRITERS: SARAH BRILL (WA), ALISON LYSSA (NSW), SUSIE BROMFIELD (VIC) AND ANNI FINSTERER (VIC) SPEAKING ABOUT THE DEVELOPMENT OF THEIR WRITING. ALL OF THESE WORKS HAVE ALREADY OR WILL SHORTLY HAVE FULL-SCALE WORKSHOPS AND READINGS.*

DANCING WITH ANGELS
Susie Bromfield

> *OPENING MUSIC* BLOOD ON THE MOON *BY ANDRÉE GREENWELL FROM SIDETRACK'S* FRIGHT, *LYRICS BY KEITH GALLASCH*

This play is about a person's search for his place in the universe set amidst the chaos of a rapidly disintegrating psychiatric institution. I see the set as minimal and fluid. Scene changes are rapid and where possible, a scene may commence prior to the ending of the scene preceding it. I'd like to thank Playworks for the nurturing support without which this script would have remained where it was—in the bottom drawer.

AN DEN WASSERN ZU BABEL *FROM ARBOS BY ARVO PART. STARS IN A NIGHT SKY. ADRIAN STANDS ALONE CONTEMPLATING THE NIGHT SKY.*

Adrian:

My father said: Let me show you the universe.

His hand is big. It enfolds my hand. His hand traps my hand in his. Maybe he'll take me to the top of the world, I think. Maybe it's my turn to die. The wind hits my face; my hand is trapped in my father's hand. With his other hand he points to the night sky. We walk towards the edge of the cliff. My foot touches a stone, kicks it over the edge.

I hear it clatter, then drop into the sea. The sky, my father is saying, there is nothing like the sky at night. Listen. I listen but all I can hear is the wind crackling through dead grass and the ocean's roar and my father's voice above and away with wind naming and explaining. I wait. I can feel the hairs on my legs bristle and goose bumps grow.

And then my father grabbed me by the legs and spun me around. Around and around on the top of the cliff. I could smell the ocean then the flaky grass; ocean, grass; ocean, grass.

My father clasped my legs tighter and spun faster. Around and around on the top of a cliff. I could hear his laugh. I waited for him to smash my head against a rock or pull me apart like the carcass of a rabbit. I waited for him to release his grip on my ankles and send me spinning, out over the ocean, where I would be eaten by sharks.

MORE STARS. THE AUDITORIUM IS ALIVE WITH STARS.

Look up, screamed my father's voice.
Would it kill me if I did? Would he kill me if I didn't? Would I dare to take my eyes off the ground? Was it the power of my brain working through my eyes that kept me from crashing into the ground? Could I buy time by looking up? Look up, look up! screamed my father's voice. And I raised my eyes.

THE STARS BEGIN TO SPIN.

The sky was a shining whirlpool. Stars, planets, galaxies. Millions of them. Appearing, disappearing, swirling about each other, shivering at their own beauty. And dancing. Dancing a galactic dance. My senses exploded. I could hear the hum of the stars; the whirring of Saturn's rings beyond my father's laughter. I could feel the Earth's pulse. My soul had been opened. I saw the universe.

I have never been so close to my father.

TROPICAL SCENE. A BUREAUCRAT LIES ON A BANANA LOUNGE, TWO OTHERS ARE ON DECKCHAIRS. THEY ARE ALL DRESSED IN SUITS AND SUNGLASSES AND DRINKING MAGNIFICENT CONCOCTIONS. BANANA LOUNGE HAS A SUN LAMP SHINING ON HIS FACE. DECK CHAIRS 1 AND 2 ARE VERY ATTENTIVE.

BL	Bandaged and blind.
DC1	Pardon?
BL	That's how I see them.
DC2	Bandaged and blind.
DC1	Swept under the carpet.
DC2	Hidden in a cupboard.
DC1	Locked in the potting shed.

DC2	Sent to the country!
DC1	Country rehabilitation!
DC2	Nursing homes in the country!
DC1	Nursing homes with a view!
BL	Poor beggars
DC2	Poor beggars locked in those wards.
DC1	All those years.
DC2	The pain.
DC1	The suffering.
BL	The cost.
DC2	Endless services.
DC1	Medical.
DC2	Dental.
DC1	Technical.
DC2	Funeral.
DC1	Spiritual.
DC2	Chiropody.
BL	Lips sewn together.
DC1	Pardon?
BL	Eyes unseeing.
DC2	Who?
BL	Locked in back wards.
DC1	(RELIEVED) The patients.
BL	Forgotten.
DC1	Terrified.
DC2	Unknown.
DC1	Unknowing.

...

GRAVEGNOMES

This is a monologue to be physically illustrated by a man or a woman supported by a violin. It's about a man who attacks a woman in a cemetery. I read an article in the paper about a man who had attacked statues in the Botanic Gardens, cut off all their limbs. I started thinking about the difference between vandalising a statue and raping or attacking a human being and that investigation led to this character who on the one hand protects statues and on the other attacks a woman because he can't understand what she's saying to him—she speaks Spanish.

One thing I'm interested in with my writing is in seeing performers work the text through their bodies. So that a language that is musical comes from a gestural language that can sit apart or with the dialogue. Often when I see theatre, the actors look like their heads are cut off from the bodies. I was trained as an actor that the body is a machine that works in harmony and writers need to write for that. It makes the stage a live place and asks the spectator to become more involved. Too often the theatre is a dead place. I'm not sure whose fault that is but that's the thing I want to have a go at as a writer.

Anni Finsterer

Norm:

One day—well I was walking thru as you do. You peruse and use the time for muse— when I saw before me I saw me—Aphrodite. Looming larger than life as if she had just sprung from the frothy sea. As if she had come for me! And so overcome I was I was stunned to a dead stop. Ahhh. Surrounded by em all—and goggle eyed I went gooey ... There was Cronos, Iris, Poseidon of the Sea, Hecate, Demeter, Earthmother to all and sundree, Artemis, Apollo, Athena, the gggggggggorgeous goddess of Summer. Seemed like for days I stood like a drongo droolin' in the light of ecstasy cast down by Dionysus ... until ... until I saw the details ... details—that spelled damage. Look, Norm. Look!!! So I looked. I looked hard. Close. I came close. I got closer. And it became clear that these statues 'd been havocked with!—some a limb lopped. And other with a finger or toe, a nose, go—just gone!!!

Ho how vile of the vandals who lurk in the shadows to hurt the heroes. The heroines. Hey Apollo? Some people aren't content bein' misters—ho no. They mean to be masters and 'd do any dirty deed to leave a mark on the world—well it makes 'em feel pumped up and proud!!! Hey my beauties. I wish I could pull on a wish bone and miraculously make myself a micro surgeon. I wish I wasn't just normal old Norm Nicholls with nothin' to offer ... Yeh, I said I wish we could sail away to a safe place. Where you feel well where you feel normal bein' abnormal. Like lucky old me—well I finally found me the graveyard. You gotta get your T.L.C. Everyone deserves some I reckon! Right? Not like what they'll do with youse. They'll throw you into the bin. The bloodless bin. Or smash you to the ground so you go to the statue graveyard. And all your porcelain remnants 'll be reshaped into something ... paltry—geez the heat's on here now—what'll I do? I gotta make a move! Mmmmmm. Think. Think with your thinking cap. Think. Think Think. Think thought. Think thought. Grave! I thought grave I thought yard. I thought graveyard ... I'll take youse to the graveyard!!! Yee. Yipp Yippee ... But wait—how do I cop n robber ya out of the godforsaken garden for god's sake?

I know! I got it! I'll wait for Apollo to down the sun. I'll wait for sun down an' then I'll steal in ever so secretive shhhhhh—hush my heavenlies—or there'll be hell to pay. Please—I hope like hell I can lift you big logs ... And I did! I damn well did lift the gods to celestial spheres so high in the sky I like a crane cranked 'em up and into the back of me Valiant till me mag wheels made out of there, that garden in the city, to freedom freedy!—and into the cemetery ... Isn't it magic here on Mt. Olympus?

FASHION TIPS FOR THE YOUNG AND BEAUTIFUL

1. When the kids were in bed I'd go to Mum's room and try on all her clothes, use her make up. Hours and hours I would spend in there, testing this and trying that. I'd watch her get ready, try and pick up her tricks. And magazines, endless magazines, telling me how to make my eyes bigger, my cheekbones defined and my mouth sexy.

Some nights I watched her get dressed and I'd say Mum, when I grow up I want to be just like you. And she would ruffle my hair and tell me things. Horror stories about the body and I pass it on to my girls. She would tell me it's work to be beautiful, that you can't ever let it slip and I tell my girls.

I say, girls, beauty may be something you're born with and you may think it comes natural but you've got to learn how to use it, learn how to keep it. I say, never take your beauty for granted. You forget, you look away and it'll be gone. I say, baby you turn your head and it's going to be sagging down around your ankles. And their eyes go wide with fear and they say yes Aunty Jane and they all run to the mirror to make sure nothing's been sagging while they haven't been looking.

I remember one time in that town when she never came home. All weekend she never came home. We all carried on like she was there and it's not until Wednesday that she returns. And she never says a thing. I ask and I ask and she never says a thing. And she's home all the time, and the bathroom in that house is only big enough for one woman.

I still watch my mother get dressed and I still say Mum when I grow up I want to be just like you. Only she'd hit me now, not hard or anything but I know she meant it and she'd say, you're too old to be saying that now. But I said it anyhow. I said it over and over until I wanted to be more than her.

2. Out on the street at night, I take my first girl's hand and I say, what is your name?, and she tells me it's Charmaine, and I say what a lovely name for someone with such a bad wig and she smiles at me because she doesn't yet understand what I am about to teach her. The first thing I do is put her in the bath and when she is finished and wrapped in a robe. I tell her my story. I tell her the power of beauty and the strength of style, I tell her where I am and why.

I tell her all these things can be yours, and she smiles at me sleepily. I say I am going to teach you about beauty and love and passion as she nods off to sleep. I say,

I am going to tell you about power, I am going to teach you to live forever and she mumbles, yes Aunty Jane.

3. In the morning I study Charmaine's bruises and I tell her that she thinks she has loved but bruises are not a sign of love. I say, the bruises of love can not be seen and they are slower to heal. I show her how to apply make-up to hide the ones that can be seen. I show her how to make up her face, to bring out her finer features. I tell her she is not to eat chocolate. She wants to tell me about her life but I say, no, tell me about your dreams. And she does, and then I say, now we are going to make your dreams come true ...

Sarah Brill

WHERE THERE'S A WILL

This is a serious comedy about a family who believe that if you hold on to cleanliness and order you'll never have to deal with the bad things that happen to the unspeakable lower halves of people's bodies. The play opens when the father of the family has died, leaving his wife Ruby dotty enough not to be able to manage on her own, but canny enough to know that her three adult children can't be trusted. Ruby wants to go on living in her crumbling gingerbread house on the coast not far from Sydney. The trouble is her children know the house is on a block of land that has become a developer's dream. Go up one storey and you get a view to kill for.

Cherry, the youngest of the offspring, looks on her father's death as a personal gift from the universe. She's recently turned forty, but years of earnestness as a naturopath and film-maker have not made her any money. She is determined to look after her mother. Not for the money, you understand, but because she deserves it. After all, she's the one who suffered most out of life and she's determined to prove it to the rest of them.

The scene you are about to read is taken from early in the play. Cherry has moved in with her mother, while her elder brother and sister have gone back to Sydney to plan their next moves for control of the estate. Cherry is lonely as well as broke. The opening scenes show her vulnerability to being put down by others in her family. She's hoping to make her living teaching belly dancing to abuse victims, but no-one believes she'll succeed. In the following scene Cherry tries to offer her mother a gift of truth, show her how to connect with her own body. But it's hard going. Ruby doesn't have the vocabulary for unseemly truths and she has washed from her memory the events from long ago when Cherry gave birth to her brother's baby.

Alison Lyssa

The set for Where There's a Will *is dream-like and distorted. We are in a coastal town north of Sydney, outside a fifties Australian house,* The Ramparts, *whose dimensions recall the house in* Alice and Wonderland *where Alice was trapped when she got too big.*

A giant Hills Hoist clothes line like a crazy tree breaks through the roof. If possible, characters are able to grasp an arm of the Hills Hoist and swing or else create the illusion of swinging.

From the roof a flag pole and extension of the clothesline, flies the Australian flag (the traditional Blue Ensign with the Union Jack in the corner, not a new one, should Australia change its flag). When Ginger and Cherry are children in the bathroom acting out their naked pirate fantasies, the Jolly Roger pushes the Australian Flag off the pole.

The roof has two openings—chimney and skylight—each large enough for one or two characters to pop out head and torso. Props such as a giant toothbrush exaggerate the way adult objects might appear to a child. The washing is distorted as if alive and includes underwear and other clothing, stained and patched sheets, and icons such as a giant enema device and Horace's cat o' nine tails.

Like a gingerbread house The Ramparts *may look as if you could eat it. Fragments are indeed edible. Cherry eats bits of it, and whole chunks more are able to be broken off or lifted out to look as if she has eaten them.*

Horace, the father of the house, recently deceased, is to be played preferably by a slightly smaller than life size effigy, moved and voiced by a puppeteer. The major reason for this is to provide a visual representation of Horace's psyche. From an early age he has split himself in two, so that he can keep control over himself. He manipulates himself in order to play the part in life he believes is expected of him. The effigy is slightly smaller than life to reflect his disappointment that despite his efforts he has never become as great as he believes he ought to have been.

Act 1, Scene 9

EVENING, THE SAME DAY. CANDLES, FRAGRANT OIL BURNING. RUBY IN CHAIR IN MEDITATION POSE, HANDS UPTURNED ON KNEES, EYES CLOSED. CHERRY IN SIMILAR POSE, MONITORS HER.

Ruby   *I don't know why a body has to go oriental.*

Cherry   *Put those thoughts into a big mustard balloon and watch them float away.*

Ruby   *(OPENING HER EYES) I never heard such nonsense.*

Cherry   *OK, OK, we'll get straight down to the exercises for the pelvic floor.*

Ruby   Don't tell your father.

Cherry   That's the great thing about your pelvic floors, he'll never know. You can
         practise right through your game of Scrabble. You've got three different sets
         of muscles down there ...

Ruby   I don't think we should do this.

Cherry   Trust me, mum, will you trust me?

         RUBY LOOKS AWAY.

         Do you want to keep peeing every time you sneeze?

         RUBY INDICATES "NO".

         Well close your peepers. Go on, it helps you concentrate. Breathe in,
         breathe out. Breathe in, breathe out. We're going to pull up those muscles
         one set at a time, moving from front to back.

         RUBY'S EYES FLICKER OPEN.

         Close those eyes. I'm going to do it with you. (CLOSES HER OWN EYES.)
         Are we ready?

Ruby   Aye. Ready.

Cherry   One, the muscles around the urethra, suck. And hold! Two, the vagina,
         suck and hold. Three, the anal sphincter, suck and hold.

Ruby   (OPENS HER EYES.) I don't know how you can say those words.

Cherry   (EYES OPEN). That's how come we're practising.
         When we get to the deep slow breath you're going to pull each one up
         from front to back.

         THEY CLOSE THEIR EYES AGAIN.

         Breathe in. Breathe out. Now on the breath, pull—One, two, three.
         And hold. Relax.
         And release from back to front. Three, two, one.

Ruby   (EYES OPEN.) They all let go at once.

Cherry	*And again, Pull up—one, two, three. And relax—three, two, one.*
Ruby	*I don't know how you expect a body to tell one from another.*
Cherry	*(EYES OPEN.) Things take time, Mumma.*
	(CHERRY REACHES OUT TO RUBY. RUBY TAKES CHERRY'S HAND.)
Ruby	*My Cherry Blossom.*
Cherry	*Where's the rest of the old photos?*
Ruby	*I think your father had a bonfire.*

TIMEKEEPER ANNA MESSARITI PAIRS A MOUNTAIN OF SOCKS.

ISOLATED AREA OF LIGHT AND SOUND SYSTEM FOR CASSETTE.
A WOMAN ENTERS IN GENERAL LIGHTING STATE AND
BEGINS SETTING UP TWENTY WHITE COFFEE CUPS AND SAUCERS.
SHE ASKS THE AUDIENCE IF THERE IS ANYONE WHO SMOKES.
LIGHTS UP ON AUDIENCE.
THE SMOKER IS INVITED ONTO THE STAGE WHERE SHE AND
THE WOMAN PROCEED TO LIGHT A PACKET OF INDONESIAN CIGARETTES AND
PLACE THEM ONE BY ONE ON THE SAUCER OF EACH CUP.
THEY BOTH EXIT. LIGHTS FADE. MUSIC BEGINS.
A MAN'S VOICE.
THEN THE SOUND OF A MOTOR BIKE.
DEBORAH POLLARD STANDS AMONG THE CUPS.
SHE IS DRESSED IN A VARIETY OF BATIK CLOTHS, A BASKET BALANCED ON HER HEAD.

3   3A   4

3   3A   4

mother tongue interference

I'm fine, fine, fine, terrific. Well pretty much well fine. Coping, coping coping with a capital C.

Problem, no problem, none what so ever. Saya masih gembira tidak apa apa.

Only occasionally, like yesterday, bad pang but now just fine. No what whats. Fine.

Space, no problem, space none what so ever, space that is . Don't need it, don't miss it, lots of people, lots of friends, many, many many many, many, many FRIENDS! NEVER EVER LONELY.

It's been ah, it's been ah, it's been aah six hundred and seventy five days but I always forget. Saya selalu lupa.

SLEEP, SLEEP, sleep don't need it, don't miss it, staying wired and fine with continuous noise, SLEEP, don't even like it any more. I never want to miss out on anything because there is always so much going on.

Toilet paper. Could send some, but don't miss it. Saya tidak pikir tentang Kertas Kloset.

Chocolate, send some, but don't miss it. Saya tidak pikir tentang cakalat.

Only occasionally am I searching for a cheese sandwich and really I've got it down to once a week. Very rarely the creamy dream returns pressed between two very thin, very white slices. Occasionally wholemeal with chunky bits and seeds but this passes really. Rice, rice, rice, rice , rice, rice, rice. Maaf roti sudah habis. Rice rice rice, enak sekali terirna kasib tambab lagi.

The dogs bark at me apparently I SMELL LIKE CHEESE. Fine. I haven't eaten cheese in over year but fine great terrific. Settled settled settled, adapted like a bat to a ball. Cold water bathing, my favourite wake me up. First thing in the morning, thes lhes krenim, krenim, krenim whirl , whirl, whirl, psssssssssssssssssssssssssss squat toilet, squat toilet, squat toilet.

Apparently if you stand on one leg and touch your tongue to your nose you're fine, they have assured me. Don't worry about me. Jangan khawatir. I'm completely and constantly happy. At last I've found meaning, true meaning about what it all means. I've never felt this fulfilled in my entire life.

Only occasionally once a month do I have a fortnight of uncontrollable weeping and depression. I've blended, I've got that look of I definitely belong. That lived in familiar feel. They can't tell the difference, I can't tell the difference. I'm one of the gang, the family, happy, empty, blended, settled, contented, in for the duration, no looking back, all bases covered, FINE! Small children flock around me to play with the fine blond hair on my arms. FINE!

I've even stopped sleeping with a mosquito net Buzzzzzzzzzzzzzzzzzzzzzzzzzzzzzz. Stopped taking my anti-malarials. Why? Because I have a keen and sensitive Cross Cultural Awareness.

When I walk down to the markets I only have to shout STOP LOOKING AT ME, once every visit. Why? Because I feel accepted. Home Sweet Home!

Apparently it's the involuntary wimpy noises you have to be on the look out for. But me I'm just fine, I only have a little mother tongue interference.

SHE CRIES OUT LIKE A BIRD

sunday

10:15 ᴬᴹ

15:10:1995

20   KODAK 5053 TMY   21   KOI

20   KODAK 5053 TMY   21   KOI

post gulf war writings

paula abood

At the cusp where the world prepared to enter into the nineties...

...culture shock
disoriented modernity
to interlooming resistance...

Challenging the reading/s of images and representations of 'other' cultures, *the politics of belly dancing* was part of the writings in the post-Gulf War period of the nineties.

Writing off the war was the catalyst for textualising dissent, for acting out political realities on the cultural front when in 1990/91, the Gulf came to Australia. This war, so much the modern crusade, set the scene for a decade of the new world order.

...from the desert oasis to the desert storm...

With the combined effects of television and centuries of disbelief, real life exploded in our faces as identities were called into question, loyalties demanded of Arab Australians. As CNN led a full frontal assault on identities, peoples and cultures, the image makers were intent on giving credence to this brave old racism.

Transcending the absurdist realities of that intense period, Sydney Arab women acted up on the streets in protest and in performance. Coming from experiences of being compelled to speak directly to this so called difference, to detonate political misunderstandings, activisms required radicalised difference. We had to find new ways of working through the layers.

Two productions in the heady days of 1991 saw the emergence of a new performance language addressing specific political, social and cultural issues affecting Arab Australians. Death Defying Theatre produced *Cafe Hakawati* a compelling bilingual performance in response to community experiences and realities in Western Sydney. Here, the diverse voices of Arab Australians challenged the monosyllabic sounds of the so called experts dealing in stereotype and prejudice, and countered talk of smart bombs and collateral damage of the virtual war.

In 1991, Sydney based Arab Australian theatre group, TAQA presented *Al Qamaraya* (The Moongate), a bilingual surrealist work examining identity, dislocation and bi-culturality. In 1993, TAQA produced ... *and they called her silence* using political magic realism to explore the poetics and complexities of sexuality, gender, culture and form.

In all of this work, the thinking, writing, producing and performing was developed collaboratively by TAQA members. Significantly, the breaking down of literary/cultural representations of Arab women and Arab culture has been a focus, as has locating the self as subject in these works. By interrogating performance practices in the public space, TAQA contributes to a more critical understanding of difference in the landscape of contemporary Australian theatre.

The artists collaborating in *the politics of belly dancing* (1993/94) continued to pursue these ideas. An alliance of Sydney women from Arabic background (SAFA) came together for this project, developing text, movement and sound for performance in Sydney and at the National Festival of Australian Theatre in Canberra.

the politics of belly dancing actively challenged the notion of orientalism, its global and local applications, with a particular focus on representations in multicultural arts practices.

...trafficking in culture
the trick of this trade
curator of the orient
exploring intrigue...

The dance form provided the structural relief to explore issues of gender, culture and appropriation.

...still the stories fetishise the landscapes
with sexuality
and violence...

As the boundaries shift uncomfortably inside and outside the margins, the ambivalence towards a critical multiculturalism remains. While we might recognise the degrees of freedom allowed Arab Australian artists, we are painfully aware of the differences in understanding/s, and of the political nature of representations. We will always be compelled to find creative ways to speak to the compounding indifference out there through performance practices that address the complexities of understanding, and not understanding.

did you hear the sultan pardoned the sultana
and she danced the night away

did you hear they raped and occupied the land
and she danced the night away

did you hear they shot the belly of the woman
who threw the seven stone
and she danced the night way...

ANOTHER VOICE BREAKS THE DARK:

Where're ya from, love?

ON THE VIDEO SCREEN, A WOMAN IN A VEIL.

PA   *I'm Australian.*

JACQUIE LO SLOWLY REMOVES HER VEIL.

JL   *Yeh, but where ya really from? Where're ya people from?*

PAULA DOESN'T ANSWER.

JACQUIE LO

Cultural difference is a two-edged sword. It's important to reclaim and celebrate non-mainstream cultures–less than twenty years have passed since the White Australia Policy–especially for women of non English speaking background who tend to have less of a public voice.

But emphasis on difference per se runs the risk of essentialism (eg all Muslim/veiled/Asian women are repressed). Our insistence on the validity of our difference often leads us to look to convenient signifiers of difference–language and food ... a small step from falling back into the trap of "souvenir culture"–exotic, non-threatening and easily pushed onto the fringes of "real Australia".

We (which me?) like this palatable multiculturalism–tabouleh, bocconcini, sambal oelek, a spice rack to enhance the steak and two veg diet. But when plans are underway to build a mosque in prime real estate Campbelltown or Arab-Australians congregate to make sense of the Gulf War, "allegiances" are questioned; multiculturalism is seen as having "gone wrong" or "too far" and words like "ghetto", "ethnic" and "ingrate" leave a bitter taste.

The underside of multiculturalism is more difficult to negotiate both externally (to the "centre") and within distinct non-English speaking/migrant communities. What do artists, community activists and educators do when our "own kind" fight, cheat and exploit each other? When ethnic groups compete for ascendancy on the multicultural hierarchy? When our ethnicity becomes the passport into our chosen field, rather than any appreciation or understanding of what we are really trying to say and do?

Communities are mythic constituencies based on shifting allegiances and modes of identification. When does "we" become "they"? Will my mad dance within the hyphens of a Chinese-Malaysian-Australian persona become mere routine one day? How can I sustain the practice of critical multiculturalism and hang on to the uneasy tension between self and other, them and us?

It will be interesting to monitor awards and funding for multicultural arts in the post-Demidenko period. I think increasingly we'll be asked to prove our ethnic/cultural authenticity now that the first bloom of romance with official multiculturalism has faded and its difficulties are foregrounded. A pessimistic prognosis–multiculturalism will veer away from an exploration of the hybrid space of say, Chinese-Australian-ness or Arab-Australian-ness and focus instead on defining and reifying differences, promoting monoculturalisms.

The tendency to essentialise cultural differences is also clearly present in institutional practices like education (it's easier to teach ancient or traditional Asian arts, for instance, than contemporary hybrid works) and in arts criticism. *the politics of belly dancing* was criticised by one journalist as "suffering from its own authenticity" which I take to mean that despite being performed and produced by the Arabic community, the politicised and deconstructionist mode of production confused the expectation of a tit-tilating belly-dance performance.

To be effective and constructive, performances of difference must be grounded in social and material contexts. *the politics of belly dancing* didn't just rehearse the plea for tolerance and equity but looked at post-Gulf War Australia and the lived reality of some Arab-Australian women in Sydney. It ranged from traditional myths and their contemporary forms to dramatising the experience of walking down the streets of Sydney in a veil at the height of the Gulf War. This concern with the everyday, the now rather than the mythic exclusiveness of a "homeland" challenges more conventional and dominant representations of multicultural arts.

VENETIA GILLOT IS A THEATRE DIRECTOR, DRAMATURG, CULTURAL WORKER, WRITER AND PERFORMER.
BORN IN DURBAN SOUTH AFRICA, SHE MIGRATED TO AUSTRALIA IN 1976.
THE SEQUENCE OF EVENTS IN SOUTH AFRICA SHE OUTLINES IS FROM APARTHEID,
A DOCUMENTARY FILM, PONT DU JOUR, FRANCE 1992.
SHE READS FROM HER LAPTOP COMPUTER.

VG *Sorry, no time to print.*

▷ 4A 5 ▷ 5A

▷ 4A 5 ▷ 5A

the return

venetia gillot

The wheels hit the tarmac at Sydney International Airport. It's 10 pm on Sunday 1st October, 1995. I feel the jar of landing in a 'new' place go through my body and then many resonant jars over the next two weeks with ten other women in *The B-File* Workshop. Airlines have lessened the discomfort of landing on new ground and technology has helped cushion the impact. How will we deal with strange new territories in the theatre?

Exile makes one fall silent/earth (taire/terre). But I don't want exile to make silence. I want it to make earth; I want exile, which is generally a producer of silence, extinction of voice, breathlessness, to produce its opposite.

Héléne Cixous

SOUTH AFRIKA, 1985.

Television allows the whole world to see how life is at Sharpville, Soweto and in more than thirteen other districts.

The repression is as brutal as ever, but now it takes place under the eye of the camera. The country is shown daily to be in flames.

Economic sanctions start to bite.

The Stock Market collapses.

Business circles become seriously concerned and conclude that Botha's program is doomed to failure.

Negotiations with powerful business and leaders of the ANC.

By the end of 1985, the wall of Apartheid is starting to crumble. The Pass Laws or Dompass (Stupid Law), which has put seven million blacks in prison, is abolished.

A new culture of resistance emerges. Workers organise.

Trade unions take to theatre as a means of getting their message to the people.

These are the years that see the birth of the 'Toi Toi',
the dance that imitates the gestures of the guerilla fighter.
A dancer leader calls the tune and the group responds.
Thousands 'dance' their resistance in the street.

ADELAIDE, 1985.

I have graduated from my theatre and film course at university. I am involved in
the development of 'dance narrative' with Julie Holledge and John Romeril for
The Kelly Dance.

I attend my first South African Solidarity meeting in years. The burning anger in the
pit of my stomach went away one day. Only by its absence am I aware of its presence.
I have been terrified of its return.

A woman from the ANC speaks of the working conditions for black women—mainly
domestic servants. I begin to weep. Unable to stop, I leave the meeting.

Australians, it seems to me, do not relate to collective tragedy. Once they are able to
sympathise on an individual level, they understand the rest. I go home and days later,
write a monologue in an attempt to use my life, my voice, my body as a bridge so that
the larger experience may be understood. For years, I show it to no one.

A Conversation About Alice (Excerpt)

ZABET
You can't be!
Amie, tell me you're joking
Alice's daughter? My Alice?
The Alice I've been talking to you about ad nauseum?
Except she wasn't my Alice at all, was she?
She was ... Mathunda ... your mother.

I knew nothing of Mathunda
Yet I told you all I knew of Alice.

Alice's Back.
Alice's Breast.
Alice's Lap.
Alice's Room.

Whenever there were happenings
Not for the eyes and ears of little people
It was to Alice's room that my sister, Sybil and I were banished.

When my mother went into labour with the twins
And they carried her out to the ambulance on a stretcher
Alice let us peep through the crack in her door.

Alice explained.
Nobody else did.

Do you hate me Amie?
You must hate me.
'Course, I had three mothers
Ouma, Mum and Alice
And you? Who did you have?
Little mother at nine to two littler ones.
No joys and comforts of childhood for you.

No, you were scared shitless every time you lit that primus stove
To boil the water for the much-diluted powdered milk bottle.
Three times a day you carried the water
From the communal tap in the township
Scrubbed your sister and brother clean
And dressed them in the castoffs of my brothers and sisters.

No fluffy towels and talc
No mother's breast to comfort you.

Alice returned to the township every Saturday
"Where are you going, Alice?" we'd ask.
"Home"
"Aaaah. Why?"
She never said why.
She disappeared on Saturdays and reappeared on Mondays
For ten years.

Then one Monday she didn't come back.
"Where's Alice?"
Nobody knew.

"This is not at all like her, you know" worried Ouma.
"Something must be very wrong."

For days the conversation revolved around Alice's absence.

"Do you think we should check the hospitals in Bazil?
Or the mortuary? Where does one start?" asked my mother at a total loss.

No address. No telephone.
Only name, tribe and township on the reference book my parents
were obliged to produce.
Every time the police chose to turn up in the middle of the night
And bang on Alice's door.

"No use worrying. She's bound to turn up," said Dad.

And us kids couldn't fathom how life was supposed to go on as normal.
"Who's going to bath us?"
"Who's going to take us to kindy?"
"Who'll do the washing and the ironing and sweep the yard?"

King Edward V Hospital. Outpatients.
A young white intern fills out a form.
30th April 1959. Bantu. Male. Infant. Dead on Arrival.

"I don't know why you people always wait until it's too late."

You told me that story not long after we met, Amie.
When Josie had that bad attack of gastro. Remember?

You told me how your mother had arrived home
To find your baby brother limp as a rag.
How she'd wrapped him in a blanket and travelled with him
on the buses from the township to the hospital for three hours.
Then stood in the Outpatients queue for another five
She didn't know how long she'd been carrying a dead child.

Alice! Alice! Where have you been?
Ouma took one look at her and shooed us out of the house.
They sat in the kitchen talking for a long time,
Drinking sweet black tea and eating vetkoek.

That conversation changed your life.
We both know that now.

Just as we both now know that the old lady who put you through high school
and varsity with her winnings on the gee-gees
Was my grandmother. Crafty old witch.
Paying for her sins. Or the sins of her father more like.

When did she realise, Amie?
Are you going to speak to me, or did you just come over
To watch me squirm?

In Natal, war erupts between the United Democratic Front and the Inkata Movement.

Before fighting begins, there are 'magic preparations'.
The Zulu warrior scars his face, arms and back with a razor blade.
He douses himself with the branch of a tree dipped in water,
jumps through a circle of fire, and is on his way.

The ritual of 'necklacing' begins. This is how the traitors die,
the ones who collaborate with the whites.

Since the written and audiovisual media is spreading images of violence,
since world opinion is shocked by what it sees,
there will be no more images.

The ritual of burying the dead takes on new meaning. And when the funeral is over,
the police disperse the crowd, fire their guns, give rise to more funerals.
Toi Toi and funerals turn and turn about.
Most of the people are under twenty years of age.

ADELAIDE, 1986.

I research, dramaturg and direct a work which explores the rites of urban mythology,
teenage sexuality and suicide (*The Last Drive-in on Earth*).

SOUTH AFRIKA, 1987.

The White Tribe of Afrika rise up and chant their chant for Apartheid.
A general strike is called. Botha grants a free hand to his security services.
State killers are given licence to track down their victims,
even those in exile ... murders, bombs, parcel bombs.

ADELAIDE, 1987.

Caryl Churchill's *Soft Targets*—the civilian casualties of war. I direct a production raising
awareness about people living with AIDS.

SOUTH AFRIKA, 1988.

July 18. Today is Nelson Mandela's 70th birthday. The world sings for his freedom.
The mother of Afrikan song, Miriam Makeba,
28 years in exile, makes heart rending music at Wembley Stadium.

ADELAIDE, 1988.

The icon of Australian women's song Robyn Archer writes a play in collaboration with some black women from Australia, Ghana, America and Jamaica (*Akwanso Fly South*). I am invited to be her assistant. I am filled with joy ... my first chance to work with my black sisters in twelve years ...

SOUTH AFRIKA, 1989.

In Europe, the Berlin Wall like the Wall of Apartheid is tottering. The Communist era is reaching its end and Perestroika is the catchword. A "new world order" is being prepared.

Botha is forced to resign. F. W. De Klerk is elected President.

Elections are called for Whites, Coloureds and Asians. Coloureds and Asians boycott the elections in solidarity with Blacks. The old divide-and-rule isn't working any more.

Civil disobedience campaigns are organised. Purple rain. Purple people's power. Child guerillas are buried. South African mothers wail.

ADELAIDE, 1989.

I am freelancing. I have my first taste of extended periods of unemployment. I volunteer to work on the First International Indigenous Women's Conference. I meet indigenous Australian playwright Eva Johnson and the experience of exile is our common ground.

SOUTH AFRIKA 1990.

The dismantling of Apartheid begins. Nelson Mandela is set free after 28 years in prison. The ANC begins negotiations with the Nationalist Government.

South Afrikan police propel the violence between Inkata and the ANC. 3,200 people die in one year. Death squads assassinate key ANC figures. Mandela breaks off negotiations.

ADELAIDE, 1990.

I work with Eva Johnson on her one woman show around issues of sexual and racial identity, *What Do They Call Me?* There are just the two of us on this project. We delight in the freedom and the control. We weep with laughter, pain and rage. We want to hit out at everyone and everything. We want to heal and reconcile and find peace. On the opening night at the Lesbian Festival in Melbourne, Eva is a pussycat. She has decided on reconciliation. The audience approve. She receives a standing ovation. After her performance, she gives out free copies of the book, *Survival in Our Own Land*. The next day in the Melbourne Town Hall, I shake hands with Nelson Mandela.

SOUTH AFRIKA, 1991.

De Klerk, Mandela and Buthelezi meet for a Peace Accord.
They begin drawing up a constitution.

DARWIN, 1991.

I head for the Top End of Australia. A new life, a new culture, a new environment, or maybe just a return.

The first show I direct in the Northern Territory, Suzanne Spunner's *Spilt Milk*, is banned by the Education and Arts Minister. This is a return in more ways than one. Undaunted, I write with June Mills, an adaptation of *The Mountains of Tibet* and direct *Muppulbah*, the first Aboriginal youth theatre production in Darwin.

SOUTH AFRIKA, 1992.

68% of Whites vote in a referendum to end Apartheid.

DARWIN, 1992.

I visit, workshop and research in remote Aboriginal communities across the Top End with Eva Johnson for a show we're devising. This is her first return to Crocker Island, the mission station she was forcibly taken to as a child of three.

Spirals within spirals ... beginnings and endings. Past, present and future run indefinably around each other, intersecting at seemingly random points.

SOUTH AFRIKA, 1994.

First free elections in South Afrika. An ANC government is elected.

DARWIN, 1994.

Celebrating victory with Tanzanian actor Sheila Langeberg. We create a scene in the lobby of a Darwin hotel. We record an Afrikan call and answer chant I have written for Salt Fire Water cross cultural performance group there and then.

I have lived in Australia for twenty years. In that time, the theatre has become for me surrogate 'mother' country and surrogate language ... the landscape against which to tell stories, and the language with which those stories are told. It has become a place to speak a common language with other exiled and searching spirits ... a place of refuge, a space within which to explore the rites of courage, learning, conflict, trust, endurance and vulnerability. It is a place to record, re-tell, make and remake history.

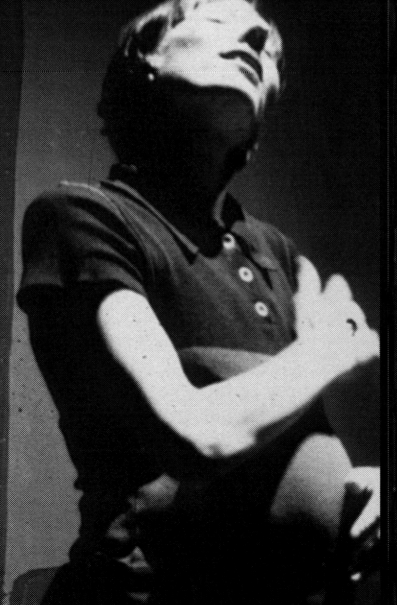

watch

victoria spence

A NOTE ON THE PERFORMANCE

This piece began its life as a piece called Waiting that was created for the 25 Years of Performance Art event at The Performance Space in 1994. Waiting was re-worked and performed as And again waiting at the Institute of Modern Art in Brisbane later in 1994. Waiting was written a month after the death of my father and was a stream of consciousness piece entirely specific to that event and to the time in which it was written. The piece was about what was to come, about the grief that I could smell but not taste. It was written from within shock, the voice of the piece is childlike, innocent, lost. The piece wove together a series of beginnings in the form of personal anecdotes that could find no end, it was about the beginning of something upon the end of another. The poignancy of Waiting depended very much upon the fact that it was performed from within my community, from a place in which my brief history as an artist was known, at least to some. And again waiting was slightly reworked for the context of a Brisbane audience that was not so familiar with me or my work.

Watch was written from a space of desperation. It charts the emotional journey that was not embarked upon in Waiting. It began where that piece ended, with the popcorn misplaced in the movies metaphor. The piece was about learning to see in the dark and was an attempt to map, in the form of images and metaphor, from within language the territory that I had traversed through my grief. By this time my father's death had become the deaths of many other significant people in my life. It was no longer the immobilising horror of death that concerned me but rather, conveying the scope of the journey that I found myself on and my inability to reassemble and string together anything by way of knowledge, certainty and meaning that I could use as a yardstick or road map.

Watch is written to be performed, not read, and so the page is littered with the most banal of conjunctions—ands and buts. These are the breath of the piece. The sense of breath in the piece is that it is delivered from underwater, that the breath is held or stolen from brief moments of resurfacing, therefore, the vocalisation of the piece works against the rhythm with which it is written. I have deliberately omitted the majority of punctuation marks from the page and instead left space, preferring to leave the experience of this piece open to the discretion of the reader. For my performance, it was entirely idiosyncratic and try as I might, I could not visually represent it on the page. Perhaps that is a shortcoming of my 1970s education, that it did not include enough attention to grammar and so my use of pause is entirely arbitrary. Thank you PLAYWORKS for your phone call. This piece was written under quite adverse conditions and I was not terribly happy with it and as such did not think it worthy of publication. Having looked at it with the sanctity of distance and yes, the passage of time, my view is now more generous.

Victoria Spence

WATCH
Victoria Spence

*A TABLE IS SET WITH A VASE OF UNOPENED GLADIOLI (RED), A MICROPHONE AND
A GLASS OF WATER. ENTER DRIPPING WET INTO THE CONFERENCE LIGHTING STATE,
SIT DOWN AT TABLE, POUR A GLASS OF WATER, DRINK IT, LOOK UP AT AUDIENCE AS IF
TO BEGIN DELIVERING A PAPER, SMILE, LIGHTS SNAP TO BLACK, HOLD SILENCE. SOUND OF
BREATH INTO MICROPHONE—PERHAPS TEARS, SWALLOWED LAUGHTER. TONE IS SLIGHTLY
APOLOGETIC. LIGHTS FADE UP SLOWLY (SO SLOWLY THAT IT'S ALMOST IMPERCEPTIBLE),
ONTO TABLE DURING THE PIECE, FROM THE SECOND PARAGRAPH OR SO.*

*i'm sorry this is all i've come up with. i know this is Playworks' tenth anniversary confer-
ence and i would have loved to come up with something a little more spectacular, at least
i would have liked to be in light but you'll have to bear with me this is the best i can do
you see i'm really tired, and a bit confused, i keep falling off my tracks, there's too much
happening in the moments, nothing is the same it's always moving and it's stuck   i
couldn't find a place to put it down somewhere safe, somewhere where i knew i could
leave it   just for a moment and that used to be exciting and now it's not   i can't make
friends with what it means any more, it's this   thing that's just too far*

*like i went to the movies and accidentally put my popcorn under someone else's seat and
when i reached for it, it wasn't there   it just wasn't there   where i left it, in its spot it was
gone, i'd put it somewhere and all of a sudden   somewhere was the wrong   place and
i didn't know if it was mine any more or   if it ever was, i didn't know if i could look for it—
if i was allowed to or   what i would find if i went looking but of course i had to go, it's
only popcorn   it can't just disappear so i thought it must be close   i'm just not looking
hard enough   not reaching far enough so i bent over forwards—to have a look, but it was
dark in the pictures   i couldn't see i had to feel (but) my arms they weren't long enough
and my legs got in the way and so i crawled. i was trying to be quiet so i didn't cause any
fuss for the people who had paid to see the movie but then the lights went out completely
and the movie started to roll and I wasn't in my seat—'cause i was calling to my popcorn
underneath   and i'd gone in way too far—i was on my own now in my guts and everyone
else was laughing 'cause the movie was really funny but i didn't get the joke i couldn't see it.*

*i was swimming on my belly in the blackness trying to find the place that i had left and
i didn't have my goggles they were in my bag on the seat that was gone and i was waiting
for the wall so that i could make the turn,   it never came   it must be soon   i'll just swim
faster out to see   oh but the waves they just got bigger, and my flippers   couldn't flip and
i was getting really tired that i couldn't stay afloat   i rang my brother,   said   i can't find
my popcorn   i think i'm going under and i don't have time to pack   i was lying on my
back on the bottom, it was cold, i didn't have my jumper and i was waiting for the whistle
to signal the final lap   i was sure i'd gone the distance.*

*(i was) wading through the sand in my gumboots like a trojan with a knapsack on my back
i was searching for the current so that i could hitch a ride but the movie wasn't over   and
i had lost the plot completely   so i plodded on regardless in the pitch (and)   i could smell
the credits rolling as the whistle found its voice and the fish began to sing (final breath)
i could hear the popcorn screaming that the current was on its way (and) the shore was
really close (and) i was riding on the wash dodging all the dumpers as the tube began
to form and the waves began to break they spewed me on the shore in a splintered
mass of seaweed*

am i breathing? are you with me? did you follow?
i drowned myself in tears, this is what i've come with, is it time yet? am i up?

SHE MOVES SLIGHTLY FROM TABLE, LIGHTS UP TO 60% AND ON LAST LINE HOLDS FOR
A BRIEF MOMENT. QUICK FADE TO BLACK.

AS SHE EXITS THROUGH THE AUDIENCE, SHE IS INTERRUPTED BY SARAH MILLER.
SHE STOPS AND LISTENS, THEN LEAVES THE THEATRE.

11:50 PM ━━━━━━━━━━━━━━━ interruption

STAGED FRIGHT

When I think about an interruption—it must be my petit bourgeois upbringing—
it sounds rude—bad mannered. "Don't interrupt when someone else is speaking.
It's not nice". Of course, I do it all the time—being nice to myself ...? I interrupt because ...
of the imperative to keep up; to keep up with what—the subtext of a conversation; in a
precipitate rush towards meaning; to capture *that* moment; to disagree (being disagree-
able); to provoke; to show off (I understand); I'm only half listening (I don't understand).

To consider/to plan an interruption—a performative gesture; to intrude on someone else's
performance—it's a concept that fills me with alarm. *Playing With Time.* Everyone seems
confident, witty, thoughtful. I don't know what to do; how to approach the moment. I am
amazed that the antagonism which so often pervades relations between those working in
'legit' theatre and other presumably illegitimate and promiscuous performance practices,
seems absent here. I'm unsure how to understand this. I worry that I'm habituated to an
outmoded polemic. I still don't know how to interrupt—only when.

This performance by Victoria Spence takes place in blackness. She offers an experience—
fragmentary, poignant, contingent. I know, because she is my friend, that it comes from
her grief—another cause for anxiety. Nonetheless, I feel I'm disproportionately fearful of
this interruption—anxious not to breach some kind of performance etiquette; something
to do with *my* history. This anxiety has assumed adolescent proportions. As Vicki leaves
the performance space, I stop her.

I interrupt—literally. I feel crass. I am loud. It is an interruption in the most conventional
sense of that term. I query the 'logic' of performance—the ephemeral nature of the
experience. I am trying to utilise various arguments (for and against) that have been
brought to bear on diverse performance practices over the past ten years. I want to be
ironic. I wish I was witty. I feel out of control and utterly self-conscious. It seems to
take a long time. I see Vicki's expression change. I'm hating this and I'm convinced that
she'll hate me. She leaves and I don't see her for days.

Sarah Miller

THE TIMEKEEPER,
ANNA MESSARITI SWAPS SOCKS FOR TOME,
TO LEAF THROUGH THE ANTHROPOLOGY OF THEATRE

3 TMY   7   KODAK 5053 TMY   8

3 TMY   7   KODAK 5053 TMY   8

(re)marking time

suzanne spunner

CAST:

THE DIRECTOR WHO READS THE WRITER—Lisa Dombrowski
THE ACTOR WHO READS THE TEXT—Meredith Rogers
THE WRITER WHO PRESENTS THE PAPER—Suzanne Spunner

THE DIRECTOR SITS COMFORTABLY AT THE TABLE AND READS.
THE ACTOR STANDS IN THE SPOTLIGHT ON THE OPPOSITE SIDE AND READS.
BETWEEN THEM IN THE DARK IN THE SHADOWS,
THE WRITER SITS CROSS-LEGGED ON THE FLOOR WITH
REAMS OF BLANK PAPER IN FRONT OF HER.
THEIR DIALOGUE IS PUNCTUATED RANDOMLY BY HER GESTURES WITH THE PAPER.
THE WRITER IS PREOCCUPIED WITH THE PAPER. IT MUST BE COLLATED,
SORTED ARRANGED, FILED.
THE WRITER DOES NOT SPEAK UNLESS SHE IS INTERRUPTED.
SHE HOPES SHE IS INTERRUPTED.
IT WOULD BE A RELIEF... TO TALK.

THE DIRECTOR: Her element is paper or so it must be, blank paper—she must love its snowy whiteness and the midnight blue of the blinking screen. She thinks of paper, and laundry images come to mind—sheets and nappies. Is there no end to a domestic way of seeing?

PAPER GESTURE ONE

For her the beginning and end is paper. In the middle is not the shadow, but the spotlight on the show, where the paper must not be revealed but masked by performance, like a balaclava on a hold-up merchant, as if there never was any paper. Words must come from lips as if never went in through eyes. Bodies move with words as if handling weapons for the first time. Gingerly. Off the paper, the words rub and bump.

PAPER GESTURE TWO

In performance, paper is dirty, out of place, superfluous or it ought to be, a reminder of the grubby making, of what was not said, thought or felt.

PAPER GESTURE THREE

I love paper, I could lie on its cool crisp white sheets. Shall I lie or loll or lounge on it?
I am washed up on its shores like driftwood rolling in the shallows.

PAPER GESTURE FOUR

Her element was paper, her enemy was time. But what was it—on paper, *en papier*,
if paper represented space then time was intense, dense, tense, a change of tense from
being to was, from might have been to could have been, or was it the revelation of an
action that could not be put into words or if put into words not shown by sleight of hand.

PAPER GESTURE FIVE

To think of ten years of time in her life, her work was not long enough and too long to
haul herself to a vantage point from which there was both prospect and retrospect.
Time could not look two ways. It was here, now or never, gone forever.

PAPER GESTURE SIX

I have always rushed time, harried it, eager to grow up, become A WOMAN, I always
wanted to be thirty-five and stay there, so it was all move on, move out, move up,
be done with this, tackle that, what's next? And suddenly the ocean of time ahead
had emptied. So no more of that!

PAPER GESTURE SEVEN

Now I want to stop it, slow it, hold and freeze it, but Time, being a man, is elusive and
wily, won't be pinned and surges on. I ride the wake swamped in the wash trying to keep
my head up, to see ahead...

PAPER GESTURE EIGHT

By the time I remember to enjoy the present it's gone. The potential for nostalgia is
infinite and seductive, and fear of and for the future is infectious like laughter. You never
know what started you off ... I cannot imagine the changes in my life being as vast in the
next ten years as they have been these last ten. Is this a breakdown of hope or just failure
of imagination pure and simple?

PAPER GESTURE NINE

Why have I allowed myself the exposure, the luxury of "I" so suddenly ? In the
beginning I could not say *I*, and they were always *they—she, the woman, the woman*

who, the woman who was not herself. In the beginning the hardest part was declaring oneself—one's colours—myself, showing my colours, saying I am an artist, I am a writer, I write, I write things about things. One day I might write plays about things. What things can I write about? Things I know a lot about, things I have to know about, things I want to find out about, things I can't do myself but wish I could...

PAPER GESTURE TEN

So what comes first—the statement of the problem interrogated. A play about two women artists—have it both ways—give yourself a choice, don't take sides. What is the answer? Art or commerce—is quiet sense of self enough or do you need supreme self confidence bordering on arrogance? One has, one has not. Will your work be better if you're freed of financial constraints ? One is and her work is, but is that the real reason she is a restless innovator? Which one do I want to be ? As a woman artist can I be both or neither? How do they stay friends? How do they work together? How do any of us work together? Art is a problem of relationships—the clever smarty pants one said, she thought she was talking about shapes and colours. We all knew different. They threw cakes at each other and stopped talking. We threw the book at each other and kept talking.

Not Still Lives (1962): A play about the artists Margaret Preston and Thea Proctor.

THE ACTOR: I AM /YOU ARE

Aphorism No 67. Art is the Autobiography of each individual artist.

T   *I am a big woman who feels tall and light.*
M   *I am a tall woman who feels big and solid.*
T   *I owe everything to fantasy.*
M   *I owe everything to science.*
T   *For me tables are dressing tables and card tables.*
M   *For me tables are laboratory tables and kitchen tables. And I have a work table....*

T   *We were shown together but only once.*
M   *I was an artist and a teacher.*
T   *I was an artist and I taught for a living.*

PAPER GESTURE ONE

THE DIRECTOR: Then some of us had babies, and I had to know what it meant to be a mother, was it just the same as being my mother or was there another way of being a mother, what does she look like, what does she say, how do you make a mother? Everyone knows how you make a baby but how do you make a mother, are they ready made off the peg?—well let's pull one apart and see, gosh don't they come apart easily. But what really holds them together?—urgent questions again, wanting answers. We all curse our parents including our mothers, and yet we have children. How do you reconcile this—how do you meet the mother in yourself you have rejected in order to grow up and become the mother yourself? Why will it be any different this time?

Running Up A Dress (1986): A play about mothers and daughters and sewing

THE ACTOR: THE MOTHER'S FACE-THE BABY'S MIRROR

New Mother: *They eat you up with their eyes. They just stare and stare; you are never allowed to evade their gaze. I feel treacherous when I look away—I have deserted her—she thinks.*

Grandmother: *It must be because they don't blink like we do. So you have to break off, they never will.*

New Mother: *The looking is incessant, obsessive. What is she? What will she be? Where did she come from? If I hadn't been at that very moment, that final unbearable push, I wouldn't believe I had anything to do with her coming into being. It is so hard to get hold of the idea that she exists utterly separate from me, and is inextricably part of me.*

Baby: *There she is again looking at me, questions in her eyes—she wants to know the 'I' she pursues with those intent eyes of hers. I have an advantage—I know her. She is me. She doesn't know yet, but she's catching on fast. She already knows I'd eat her up without a moment's thought. She gives and gives and is constantly seduced by my overwhelming appetite for her. I will devour her yet. All I know is hunger and relief when it's satisfied...*

Sewing Teacher: *SELVEDGE from self and edge. The edge of a piece of woven material finished in such a manner as to prevent the ravelling out of the weft. It's narrow closely filled edging, and by extension, a marginal tract, border, edge.*

PAPER GESTURE TWO

THE DIRECTOR: Time moves on and we move or rather I am moved by force of will by force of love, to follow him with the children to another place and I am asking can a woman live in two places, can she leave her children can she leave her husband can she leave the place she has made hers? If she has her love, her children and her work can she hold them all together or will they tear her apart? If these are all parts of herself, can she cut off, desert a part, what is her self that is left? Can it survive so damaged? Is it stronger to go than to stay?

The Accompanist (1987): A play about the musician and social activist, Hepzibah Menuhin.

THE ACTOR: THERE IS NO HEPZIBAH

Miss Menuhin:. What is the stereotype of a good woman? Look like a girl, act like a lady, think like a man, work like a dog. I am not referring to myself. Girl, Lady, Man, Dog—I am not speaking about myself. I am not here to speak of myself.

Mamina says there is no Hepzibah, perhaps she is right, for once. Who am I to say? Where has she gone? She used to live in America with a family, they loved her. She used to have a husband, children, they were a family, they loved her. My darling boys, where is your mother now? I have no mother, you have no mother, mine has disowned me as I have disowned you. I did not want to leave you, but what I wanted was so far away. What I want is so much larger and more shining than all of you, than myself, it draws me away. I need something to sweep me up. Work to fire my mind and burn into my soul, something even more pure than love, more exalted than music. I could not see it when you were all so close around me. I have been enveloped in these little families, in these little worlds, and all the time the other world out there, I don't know if it's the real world. I have to find out. There is so much cruelty, so much hatred, it cannot be shrugged off and forgotten by burying my face in your chest, Lindsay, or in the touch of their soft skin and silky hair, much as I want to, much as I have already ... much as I have, I must leave.

PAPER GESTURE THREE

THE DIRECTOR: What would it be like if there was pure total work that was one's life and all else was subsumed? There would be room for contemplation and friendship and a calm centre.

Edna for the Garden (1989): A play about the garden designer Edna Walling.

THE ACTOR: MAWARRA: AN ITALIAN GARDEN AT OLINDA

Edna   *Perhaps it will be easier for you to envisage if I show it to you on the ground. Come with me ladies.*

Miss Marshall *Well if we must, we must. Lead on Mrs. Walling.*

Edna   *We are at your front door and from here you have a fine view looking down the slope to Mount Erica. Think of this view as the grand central*

axis of my design. Then imagine a number of side axes, forming
terraces following the contours of the property. Each of these five
terraces has its own distinct character. The first terrace is behind us.
On the right are the utility areas and the kitchen garden, on the left
a birch grove and further over a swimming pool.

Miss Marshall   *Oohh, I don't know if we want a swimming pool—do you Hilda?...*

Edna   *And now for the final plunge down more steps to the focal point of*
                  this grand garden room, an octagonal pool there on the fifth and final
                  terrace. A rhododendron walk leads off from this side of the pool and
                  further over to the left of the pool are the tennis courts. There it is—
                  a symphony in stone, steps, still water and beautiful trees.

PAPER GESTURE FOUR

THE DIRECTOR: But such stillness is anathema now—it lets in too much. There's no room, no time for contemplation. Do her children determine her, or just distract and obsess her? They are like woodpeckers in her brain tapping and ticking away and if they are too quiet she worries and misses them dreadfully.

Safe n Sound (1987): A radio play about restraint and obsession.

THE ACTOR: THE MOTHER AND THE DRIVER

They swam before her eyes in the slow motion crash like weightless cherubim, angelic astronauts. The seat belts and safety harnesses that hadn't been done up, waving like fronds of seaweed caressing the tendrils of their soft hair. She heard the soundless thud of their perfect heads on the roof of the car and she saw them frozen and still through the crazed and shattered ice windows.

You can always recognise the mothers on the beach even if their children aren't in sight. They are the women with their hands and pockets full of broken pieces of glass. They can't stop themselves—even if the green and amber shards are sea smooth; at the wrong angle, they could still maim and scar unthinking running feet. So they pick them up, just in case; to be on the safe side. Mothers see themselves as the canaries in the tiny wire cages that the miners carried to check for the gas leaks. They have to go down the mine first, just in case ... they could never forgive themselves ... And they don't.

PAPER GESTURE FIVE

THE DIRECTOR: It had something to do with the children, it had something to do with love, but how did she end up here, up here so far away from what had seemed for so long to matter so much? Would she go mad and if she did would they go back, and would anyone notice her madness, their leaving. Once you leave—can you go back?

Dragged Screaming To Paradise (1988): A play about a woman who dismantles one home and makes another somewhere else.

THE ACTOR: SECOND MOVEMENT: DARWIN

She: *Oh, my God it's hot—it's an oven, a furnace-rush of hot air. It'll be all right, it must just be the heat of the engines. Walk across the tarmac, no carpeted tunnels and tinted glass here, just dusty asphalt and a wire fence with excited, eager people pushing against it.*

        I feel sick. I shouldn't have worn this dress. It was cold and raining when we left, my feet froze in sandals, I hugged my jacket round me. Now I feel my stomach contract and a wave of panic come over me. I am here. The ground is solid, hard and hot. But what have I done?

        The kids spot him, he is grinning at them and trying to look like he knows what I must be feeling. He doesn't. Take a deep breath, it'll be better inside the terminal. ... We haven't seen each other for a month but I didn't want to get out of that plane and he knows it. We let the kids take up the slack and fill the air with diversionary tensions.

PAPER GESTURE SIX

THE DIRECTOR: Seeing I'm here for the duration, better get down, get real, get local, blend in, be part of the scenery, go with the flow, no worries, enjoy the lifestyle ... get a pool!

Overcome by Chlorine (1992): a play about men, women and children and swimming pool maintenance.

PAPER GESTURE SEVEN

THE ACTOR: KICK, KICK, PADDLE, PADDLE

Geri   *Rod, just come here and put your head on my lap so I can get the drops in. Yes they do feel funny. Now turn over, so I can do the other ear. No, Rod, that way. No, no don't get up. Let it go right in. It doesn't matter—most of it went in. I'll wipe it off with a towel. Russ, hand me the towel. Thank you Russell. Don't run off. You haven't had any Blockout on yet. Just stand still, stop fidgeting! Now turn round so I can do your shoulders. Russ, stand still, you don't want to get cancer—do you? Remember what happened to Grandpa, had to have bits of his ear cut off. He did so, Rod … Gazza, what are you doing?*

Gary   *Making a whirlpool to herd the leaves into the middle. It is one of the more satisfying things you can do in this pool. Perfect corkscrew like real tornado. See! The leaves are all dancing to the top.*

Geri   *You should leave that to me, it's good exercise for firming the thighs. Hold still, Rod—Stop moving your arms I can't blow them up right if you're jiggling about. Elizabeth Taylor used to do it. It was in* New Idea—*she'd walk very fast in the water, lifting her legs as if she was marching in the surf in California or Malibu. Very good for the tops of the legs, she said.*

Gary   *Rodney poke your arms through these holes, and your head goes in the middle. The middle hole, boy. The big hole! Ger, this is too small, his head won't go through—you big Boofa Roddy.*

Geri   *Lead with his crown— smallest part of the head comes first. Same principle as giving birth.*

THE DIRECTOR: So what about a change of pace, can you hack it? The transition crunches, it hardly meshes, it's another part of the picture, alongside or just over the fence from the life in the suburbs wherever you are. Someone, in this case, he, is engaged in the problems and dilemmas of the world and I am privy to this at one remove in pillow talk so I write a play about a woman scorned and despised after her husband dies, because I want to understand what it is to look on, look over the shoulder of complex moral problems. I know what it's like to be a white adviser's wife, I can empathise with her distance from the centre and as time goes on I understand her anger, her paranoia and her isolation.

The Inkata's Wife (1990): a play about the wife of a famous anthropologist/linguist who thought he had to speak for other people.

THE ACTOR: YOU ALL THINK I AM A WITCH

I have nothing to say. Nothing to say

You all think I'm a witch—A Debbil Debbil Woman. You don't like women, do you? You think we're all witches—Debbil Debbil Women! You didn't like the Camel Girl and you don't like the Dingo Mother and you sure as eggs don't like me. You didn't like her because she was young and single and wanted to be left alone; and you wouldn't believe her because she was a mother but she wouldn't cry on cue, and you can't stomach me because I'm a widow and I won't stop grieving.

Why shouldn't I draw the curtains and stay inside out of the heat? I never liked the kitchen anyway.

... And me, I suppose you think I'm menopausal—just another hysterical woman who's past it. Past it? I won't let go of the past, won't, can't, let go ... and I will wail and lament a leviathan of wailing, buckets of tears . All gone, dead and gone!

PAPER GESTURE EIGHT/NINE/TEN

THE DIRECTOR AND THE WRITER IN UNISON: *This woman spends her life buried in an avalanche of paper which she has to keep in order. She dwells in the past, yearns for the future and cannot move because of all the time that's passed and all the paper ...*

sunday

12:35 PM

15:10:1995

KODAK 5053 TMY   3   KODAK 5053 T

KODAK 5053 TMY   3   KODAK 5053 T

go on, interrupt me

virginia baxter

VIDEO Shop (1995)

V   *Could I get some service please? Why invite me in and keep me waiting?*

A   *That wasn't me. You would have been speaking to my simulacrum. Has anyone ever told you, you have beautifully shaped lips?*

V   *Mm. I preferred her on the Virtual. Up close, I could see she was just another bad actor. The place was full of them.*

PAUSE FOR VIDEO

A   *Can I help you, madam?*

V   *Yes, seeing you dragged me into this mausoleum, I'd like some good old fashioned service.*

A   *I'm about to roster off.*

V   *This won't take a minute. I know what I want. I know what it costs. I want you to get it for me from behind that counter, wrap it, put it in a carry bag, take my credit card, thank me and send me on my way with that grimace of simulated warmth.*

A   *Colour?*

V   *Nectarine Gloss.*

A   *With your skin tones?*

V   *It retails for $25.*

A   *You'll have to wait. Our computers are down.*

V   *What d'you need with a computer? I just told you what I want.*

A   *I will need to check if that particular line is in stock.*

V   *Next thing my face is back on line—lipless!*

A   *Sorry. NLA.*

V   *What do you mean NLA?*

A   *That line is no longer available.*

V   *What now?*

A   *As you can see, madam, a universe of colour is at your fingertips. This season's story is "Genitalia".*

from *Shop*, 1995.

CUT SOUND. KEEP VIDEO RUNNING.

I am standing at a piece of furniture, part shop counter, part work station, publicly interacting for an audience with my computer, trying to sell myself on home shopping. In the performance, I can control the flow and selection of images in less than a second.

The idea that the home shopper plays saleslady to herself seemed like an interesting idea when I was writing it six months ago but in performance I realise that I have set myself a horrible task: to convincingly embody two versions of myself, two personae talking to each other while a third appears on the screen. Acting! I am lucky to escape with my life.

CUT VIDEO

I had come a long way.

INTIMATELY INTO THE MICROPHONE

Remind me to tell you about a significant moment.

Just walk, he says. Put the shoes on and just walk.
I walk. Be yourself. Just walk. Good. Stop. Again. Nice. Stop.
Now, that's you walking, not Her. We've got to find Her, he says. Think of Her.
When you're ready, open your eyes and walk and you'll be Her.

I'm in the middle of my first solo performance, *Just Walk* in 1983. I'm an actor but the Director addressing me is imaginary.

INTIMATELY Something is about to happen. *Now?*

Peta Tait (INTERRUPTER)   *Not yet.*

V   I have become a writer through a process of collaboration.

1985. I've gone autobiographical. I am writing a childhood room from memory.
The designer Lani Weedon is a painter. She sees the room as a brown and blue lino pattern that, like memory, plays tricks on the eyes. She's placed a hula hoop on the floor to my right.

I will now disappear into this room and reappear in a daring act of childhood recollection.
I will play two roles. This requires complete concentration and suspension of disbelief on the part of the audience. Please draw closer.

I pick up the hula hoop and twirl it round my wrist.

Left. Right. Left. Right. Left. Right.
The right side of things is my right wrist with the bangle.
(I tried to lose the bangle by putting my arm through the bars at the end of the bed.)
The ballerina folds down on a spring when you close the lid.
I'm collecting things that go together.

(It was a plain room. Just another part of the house.)
My room is t-h-i-s big.
Ssh! Listen. Rain on the roof.
(I never found rain on the roof comforting.)
Room's cool like ... like ... (stuck for a word.)

Linda Marie Walker (PHOTOGRAPHER/COLLABORATOR): *Go to the other end of the house.*

like ... like Mummy's hands.
She hides in here sometimes.
Lino on the floor. Curtains. Nylon. White.
(No photographs of the inside of the house. Damn!)
Blowfly! Shoo!
(Three rhymes in three frames. "House That Jack Built".)
(Cupboard under the rhymes. Shoes under the cupboard.)
My door's always open.
(My father comes in from his room across the hallway, sits sideways on my bed.)
What's up, chicken? Bad dream?
(Dreaming about hell. Mustn't say. Might come true.)
Don't turn the light off!!!
My father says: "Silly sausage! I'm gonna stand here, by this light switch here
and I'm gonna turn off this light and I want you to tell me if anything in this room changes.
OK? I'm turning the light off now. PAUSE. I'm turning it back on. OK, chicken, did anything
change?
Yeh.
What?
I did.

from *What Time Is This House?* 1985.

Later in the same performance I'll move into the audience with a set of photograph albums constructed by Linda Marie Walker from her photographs of me in my real house mixed up with the collective family snaps of the collaborators and others found in junk shops. The audience will share these albums in small groups. I'll ask them to turn the pages as I speak, reach across them and tap my finger on the surface of the pictures, drawing the audience into the frame. Suddenly they are intimates. The photos are "real".

In *What Time Is This House?* the solo performer's voice stands for my voices, the voices of my collaborators as well as total strangers—one set of house memories for part of the collective memory. A reviewer says that at one point in the performance he believes me to be a boy, which is not part of my memory. But who knows? Now?

Peta Tait

Virginia, are you in this text at all? I mean, is there a piece of the text that is recognisably autobiographical? Is it you? Or do I want it to be you, otherwise it gets too near, too familiar, too close to becoming inside?

After my students read *What Time Is This House?* as part of their course work they decide that the text is taken from the memories and thoughts of this woman, Virginia Baxter who writes and performs it. I reply it's not quite that simple and suggest they stop thinking about Virginia as a unified entity in the text and focus instead on a performance persona moving through a number of subjectivities. They argue, but why isn't it Virginia's story? After all, she says "I" all the way through the text so it must be her experience. I have to tell them that she is performing self. I tell them it's not her autobiographical self you perceive but a fake personal self. Because you assume it is autobiographical then that is how it appears. Some students hesitate, then they ask, but who is this self if it's not her, this woman Virginia Baxter?

I ask could it be you she is performing? Is she performing your personal self? No way. Well one you recognise. Maybe. Sort of. We compromise. I say, well there are fragments of a life which might or might not belong to the writer-performer and snippets of speech and phrases she or someone else might or might not have said or heard.

A sense of uncertainty pervades my conversation with the students. It becomes unsure, tentative. Everyone is uncomfortable and looks for a way out onto more solid ground. This is complicated because the exchange takes place in a pedagogical situation rather than a performance and it is extremely confronting not to know.

I proceed with my pedagogical discourse. It's safe. The text of *What Time Is This House?* is a conversation with the audience rather than a dialogue between characters. The woman appears to be speaking her thoughts aloud, interspersing colloquial phrases and recognisable sayings with confidential disclosures. She contrasts her feelings about her family with responses to people she has shared houses with, rooms with, perhaps even performance spaces. She creates the illusion of an internalised self through the presentation of fragmentary memories, alternating her responses from a childhood imaginary with an adult self. She indicates how the boundaries around her sense of self are formed by other people, firstly her family, and more recently her lover and cohabitants of her space. Her depictions of her self arise out of half-remembered conversations and the comments of other people who traverse her space.

Judith Butler writes: *"words, acts, gestures and desire produce the effect of an internal core or substance, but produce this on the surface of the body, through the play of signifying absences that suggest, but never reveal, the organising principle of identity as a cause."* (1990:134)

She asks, *"From what strategic position in public discourse and for what reasons has the trope of interiority and the disjunctive binary of inner/outer taken hold?"*

The woman in *What Time Is This House?* reiterates Butler's challenge to our belief in an internalised autonomous self. The woman in the text is performing herself for an audience as if they might know her, to show others that they can not.

I ask my students why they think there is an inner "I" which can be known. Some of them resist this thought altogether. They tell me we have an inner self because we sense it. I hesitate. I wonder, perhaps there is a solid fragment of Virginia Baxter in the text. We sense something of the real woman. If not, then what are the boundaries around performance? Where does her performance begin and end?

LIGHTS DOWN ON THE DESK. LIGHTS BACK UP ON THE TABLE.
VIRGINIA RESUMES HER PAPER.

Murder Suite, 1995. About a house, a relationship and a city being renovated. A paranoid radio serial of five five minute episodes to be played in any order written with Keith Gallasch and composer Sarah de Jong. The speech was written at the same time as the score but with no attempt to merge the two. In the studio, we play the two alongside each other and wait for the accidents. It's about architecture, insomnia and mortality.

SOUND TAPE Murder Suite

1987. The beginning of a fascination with everyday speech and the intimate patterns of couple-talk as played by Keith Gallasch and I as versions of ourselves. Surveying the politics of the heterosexual couple—not an ideologically hot topic in 1987. These dialogues are written the way we live as a couple: together and apart. We are apartners. Our company is Open City. We start with the sort of talk we perform at the breakfast table. We write with and for each other. Sometimes we forget who wrote what. Like couples, we copy and resist each other's words until the dialogues come out sounding like:

V   *Why don't you discriminate your feelings?*
K   *You're probing. Let's stick to the facts.*
V   *Probing? That's not like me at all.*
K   *Sometimes it is like you. One part of you. With a needle.*
V   *What facts?*
K   *Let's stick to what is. Feelings are messy. Thoughts are abstract.*
V   *What is 'what is'?*

K   *This room. A sound. A move through a door.*

V   *You always hit me with lists. You're drifting right away.*

K   *What do you mean 'always'? Don't you mean 'sometimes' I hit you with lists?*

V   *When it happens it feels like...*

K   *'Feels like'?*

V   *Feels like always.*

K   *When I hear 'feels like' I think 'is not actually like' or only 'seems to be' and that it will pass and you will see sense.*

V   *See sense? See sense? You're drifting right away. You've gone.*

K   *You're the one who's drifting. Not me. You're projecting your drifting onto me. That's it.*

V   *Is that a fact?*

K   *What's next?*

V   *Have we finished?*

K   *The rest is supposition. I'm waiting.*

V   *For what?*

K   *The balancing act.*

V   *Are they on next?*

K   *Your balancing act. You will apply a soothing hand to the difference between us.*

V   *And you will delete your intuitions of the worst possible conclusion to us.*

from Sense 1993, 1994.

12:50 PM   interruption

Peta Tait

That is you, Virginia. There, now? Isn't that you? I mean are you and Keith Gallasch in this text? That part of the text is recognisably you, isn't it?

VIRGINIA INDICATES YES/NO.

Recently, in America I watched a number of what they call performances and the first one I saw was a one woman show which recounted this horrific story of a father killing his son. As I was watching it I thought this story is horrendous but a fascinating and imaginative piece of writing. I was wrong. It was the performance of events in the performer's life in what seems like a repeated cathartic act of public confession. Is this a true performance of a personal self? Is it more real because it happened to the self performing it? Did I need to know this in order to watch it? Virtually all the performances I saw on that trip were recognisably autobiographical. I learned my lesson. But why did I approach this first work as a spectator who disbelieves that the text is based on actual events in the lives of the performers? Do I find it disturbing that this is the performer's experience because I am an Open City spectator? My problem is possibly cultural and definitely personal. The Americans around me never doubted that it was a "true" story by a "real" person.

In the process of viewing Open City's performances I've learned that the performance is more important than verifying the uniqueness of an individual identity or the importance of specific events in someone's life. It is the act of performance which is always being foregrounded. Doubt over authenticity of self is the pivotal problem on which the performance text balances uncertainly, precariously. The impossibility of knowing what is true is the premise behind subjective presence in this performance work.

The Open City text posits a personal self which may or may not be known. It works and re-works this trickery into a fine art. Using the most intimate revelatory style of conversation you beguile me into believing I am witness to the public act of a private disclosure, only to find you have ripped a small hole in the fabric of this conviction which keeps tearing. My belief is in shreds. Now I assume that the performance of an "I" is an inauthentic self representing an illusory "real" thing. I know it is performed. The possibility of capturing truth eludes us so we try harder. To repeat the narrative of our lives in performance sets up a truth we want to believe in. Like my students, I want to believe this is you in the text, Virginia Baxter, your real self.

LIGHT DOWN ON DESK. LIGHT UP ON TABLE.
VIRGINIA RESUMES HER PAPER.

VB   Not surprisingly, in 1995 we take to recording other people's conversations—a step away from ourselves—transcribing them, analysing them and then performing them with all their musicality (verbal tunes, backing vocals, repetitions) in a series of performances called *Talk Studio*. Language has been the key to our work but now we are putting it right on the surface.

(INTIMATELY INTO MICROPHONE) Don't forget to remind me to tell you something.

1987. Musicality. The beginning of our five year collaboration with composer Robert Lloyd on a shared interest in the relationship between words and music.

VIDEO *Tokyo Two*

WORDS WITH MUSIC

We went out into the steam
And the yellow sky
And the Tokyo crowd where you're carried along
And your eyes won't focus on anything
And it's so hot!
So this is sashimi?
I said I'm not complaining
I just said it's like eating blindfold. Jesus!
Things floated out in front of me
Kanji, knives, heat, noise
And I'm staring with my mouth open
Gasping for air. And there isn't any.
And you're saying "You're doing it. You're doing it".
What? What am I doing?
"What do you want? Twigs and kotos?
This is a modern city. There is no yellow sky.
And the crowds are not that bad."
Well ...
In the public park outside Ueno Zoo
There's a swampy pool with a few too many lotuses for my liking
and insects and zoo smells
And you're telling me the history of the area in very, very fine detail
When I swallow a beetle.
This is my first real food in Japan.
No, to me this looks like the wrong end of town.
Looks like it's been looked at too much over too many years
And it's drained of everything
Like the sky—there's no colour in the sky. It's all pollution.
And you're saying "L-o-o-k, noodle vendors", "S-e-e Sumo wrestlers"
And I can't see a thing 'cause I've blanked it all out.

from *Tokyo Two* 1992.

Tokyo Two. 1987, 1988, 1992. A couple at cross-purposes, two musicians, two cultures, two mediums (music and words), two languages (English and Japanese). And the form— like jazz. Like speaking with music, not as background but at the same time. Simultaneity. For the audience, the frame they're inside is a TV talk show. They are not sure from one moment to the next whether they're watching something real or something relayed.

I've interrupted myself.

1990. Male body interpreted through female desire. Physicality enters the realm. Two female photographers and, for the first time, choreographer Julie-Anne Long. Photographer, Sandy Edwards suggests talking to a friend of hers who's in a complicated relationship with her gym instructor. We get the story. Next day I write down as much as I remember. I write the subject as "I" (the first letter of her name—Irene). I take out the secrets, add some thoughts of my own, some of Sandy's. Then I rhythmically rearrange it. Sandy heads off to the gym with her camera. 1991.

VIDEO All That Flows. AS VIRGINIA SPEAKS TO THE AUDIENCE SHE OCCASIONALLY LOOKS IN THE DIRECTION OF THE DANCER ZORAN KOVIC WHO MOVES THROUGH A SET OF STRETCHING AND RUNNING MOVEMENTS. LEIGH GILES PLAYS BOO-BAM DRUMS AND ROBERT LLOYD PERCUSSIVELY SLAPS THE BODY OF THE DANCER. SANDY EDWARDS' SLIDES OF MEN LIFTING WEIGHTS ARE PROJECTED ON HUGE MOVEABLE SCREENS. THE AUDIENCE'S ATTENTION MOVES BETWEEN ALL THESE ELEMENTS.

So this is it, is it? Combat? OK, Well, Mr. Angel. I could say that there are better bodies than yours but it's you I like. That's all. Nothing complicated. (Tears brim but don't brim over. Don't cry!) Silence. And then I get this wild torrent.!
Just another body/What is it with women?/I only said "calories"/What do people come here for?/Therapy? Masochism? Gimme a hard time? Sick of it! Up to here!
I wait for him to come up for air and I say Maybe you're a bit hard on yourself and just a touch arrogant, like the rest of us. Arrogance is bliss, he says. The last wave. And then he sets this little paper boat of silence afloat between us. (PAUSE) So, I. went back to her lunges. Last night, she said, she dreamed about the yoga teacher again. He was sitting on me, whipping me with this little whip. And I. was this wild woman with this wild hair. And I. lifted him up like a weight in a bench press, she said.

from *All That Flows,* 1990

The real Irene in the audience for *All That Flows* told me I got the feeling exactly. On another night the man in question saw the sequence and said they were good pictures but not of his body.

Have I run out of time?

TIMEKEEPER INDICATES FIVE MORE MINUTES.

So, I have become a writer through many processes of collaboration. I write at a word processor but also through improvisation and in response to other people's creations—visual, vocal, musical, theoretical. I score words. I start from the autobiographical (taking in others' autobiographies) and I write fictions rooted in my reality. This writing gives me other voices, personae. It's a continuing investigation.

1993. A year before we programmed a computer to perform with, we began to write 'digitally'. Here, in *Sum of the Sudden*, the challenge was to write a sequence of pieces with recurring elements (a moment of loss, a couple of words, a cigarette, a man in a red shirt). These five "sudden fictions" are written to be recycled, to collide at different times during the evening with three other performances: a man in a box displaying symptoms of disorders like autism, obsessive compulsive behaviour; a woman dancing fugues in a shadow box and a couple dialoguing in very bright light about moments when ego dissolves. The members of the audience move through the performance, which begins at 7 pm and ends at 10 pm exactly, joining and leaving it as they wish.

I am standing at the end of a narrow corridor of light.

VIDEO Sum of the Sudden.

"... died in sleep ..."
Half   a message
First   and last words
Missing
I recognise the voice. I know you.
Did I hear that?
Say again. Stop!
Turn off   the light   hits
Your red shirt   stings
Where was I? Go back. Wrong way!
Go back!
Other way! She died in sleep. There!
I'm walking through water.
Dead? How? Sleep? Why there?
No. Can't be. Don't touch!
Sit. Down. Cigarette. Stop. Just stop.
Mind racing. In the dark
She who ... She who is/was ... known
to me   to us is   no more
Died in sleep
The message
Best way   no pain
Forget it! Can't see
Her lying down
For that   Not

Fair   to be
Stopped!
Just stopped!
Did she   remember everything?
in one instant   then
Forget it?
All?
Shock?
Did she dream?
SURPRISE! And her heart jump
But not wake her
Up?
Did she know too much?
Did someone take her breath   away?
I'm lost. Start again. Go back.
"...died in sleep ..."
Half a message ...

In sleep from *Sum of the Sudden,* 1993.

for Mari Shimizu

Which reminds me what I had to tell you.

1983. *Just Walk!* I am in the middle of the performance when I catch the eye of someone in the audience. I don't remember who it was. I was so interested in the look that I couldn't see. But time opened up. From that moment, I stopped acting roles and began performing myself. I started to write myself.

PETA TAIT SWITCHES HER ATTENTION TO MARGARET FISCHER
WHO IS NOW AT
THE TABLE.

KODAK 5053 TMY   26   KODAK 5053 TMY

KODAK 5053 TMY   26   KODAK 5053 TMY

a decade of writing

margaret fischer

INTRODUCTION

When Margaret Fischer performs her one-woman show *The Gay Divorcee,* there is
no doubt that she is acting a character. This performance is absolutely *not* based on the
personal and painful experience of Margaret Fischer. No performer would willingly reveal
that amount of embarrassing detail about her own indiscretions and twisted thoughts in
a play in which the woman performer comes out not only as a lesbian but as a full-blown
neurotic. Therefore, we can confidently say the woman in the text who goes to pieces
when her lover goes off with another bears little resemblance to Margaret Fischer the
cool-headed, astute and successful artistic director of the long-standing women's theatre
group, Vitalstatistix. For a start, how would she ever find the time to do all that group
therapy and healing, spending hours lying around like a mermaid in that seashell bed
on satin sheets?

Now most of the audience don't know Margaret personally. I've known her for twenty
years so I can tell you that her theatre always has a bigger cause behind it—an important
issue in a larger social context. In *The Gay Divorcee* she is clearly representing the cause
of the needy lesbian who has loved and lost trying desperately to regain her equilibrium
by having a lover. This group has been virtually ignored in social discourse and deserves
to have its specific problems properly addressed: lesbians who love too much. It was
very clever of Margie to devise a fictional character who could speak on behalf of this
neglected group in such an honest and confronting way.

As a writer-performer, Margaret Fischer knows that writing and performing actually
means doing two full-time jobs and that the term "split subjectivity" should be more
appropriately applied to women's work-based practices in theatre which enterprise
bargaining does not seem to have addressed yet.

Peta Tait

I'll begin by telling you how I got here.

I received the publicity for *Playing With Time,* looked at who was speaking, thought it
sounded interesting and then felt left out. I thought, why didn't they ask me to speak?—
after all Vitalstatistix is a *women's* theatre company and has been going since 1984.
I thought maybe it's because they've only invited women they've worked with directly;
maybe it's writers only and I haven't been a full-time writer. My friend said that she knew
Julie Holledge who was going to be part of the program couldn't go, so maybe I could
be the South Australian person if that's how people were chosen ...

My friend said "You *are* a writer and Vitalstatistix has made a huge contribution to women's writing for performance". I said, that's true. So I rang and offered myself. The organisers said, yes! I felt slightly embarrassed. So now I was the *in crowd*— because I'd rung up and asked to be.

I often feel like an outsider, an outlaw, a renegade; yet I love recognition, approval and respect. I have always wanted my work to be popular and accessible; and I am an intellectual.

I am currently the Artistic Director of Vitalstatistix, a women's theatre company based in Port Adelaide. Ollie Black, Roxxy Bent and I formed it in 1984 and it's been continually evolving over the past eleven years, producing fourteen new plays written, directed and designed by women. These writers include Tobsha Learner, Andrea Lemon, Roxxy Bent, Teresa Crea, Anne Brookman, Darrelyn Gunzberg and Ollie Black. Directors include Noëlle Janaczewska, Venetia Gillot, Rosalba Clemente, Andrea Lemon, Anne Brookman, Roxxy Bent, Sue McClements, Christina Totos and Catherine Fitzgerald.

Our Winter Playreadings held over three years have included plays by Sheila Langeberg, Mardi McConnochie, Marion Hoenig, Anne-Marie Mykyta, Cathy Clarke, Sheila Duncan, Kerry Saunders, Corrie Hoskings, Julie de Lima, Verity Laughton, Tobsha Learner, Roxxy Bent, Anne Brookman, Rosalba Clemente. Designers include Giselle Mellis, Cath Cantlon, Kathryn Sproul, Lisa Phillip-Harbutt and Kerry Reid.

Vitalstatistix has produced play readings, cabaret, festivals, community theatre, in-theatre productions, indigenous arts festivals. We've toured to every state in Australia, produced two videos, published books of our plays, lectured, worked as consultants, delivered workshops and presented the work of interstate companies to South Australian audiences, including Death Defying Theatre, Radclyffe Theatre, Women on a Shoestring and Melbourne Workers' Theatre.

We have a fantastic venue at Port Adelaide, 20 minutes out of Adelaide, a working class dockland area with a rich, gutsy history. Our venue, "Waterside", was built by the Waterside Workers Federation in the 1920s as an entertainment venue for working people. Vitalstatistix continues this tradition of popular theatre. We've carried out major renovations on the venue to turn it from an empty shell to a vibrant, flexible performance space.

We've had a remarkable decade. I could go on but I'm actually here to talk about my writing. Before I do, I'd like to draw your attention to my jewellery, a gift. I like to think of them as my medals—a designer nappy-pin with a series of diamante stars earned over the last twenty years as professional theatre worker. I'll explain their significance later.

In 1984-85 Roxxy, Ollie and I had lots of energy and vision. We'd just begun. We were group-devising with Anne Brookman who went on to direct our first play *Weighing It Up* (which is now published and performed all over Australia). Issues were what it was all about then, not like now when issue-based theatre is a complete no-no. In my view, every piece of theatre is issue-based. I've just read a two page spread about Daniel Keene in *The Bulletin*. The article focuses on his play about Bosnia and he speaks about the issues of war and the rape of women and how complacent we all are, how he wrote the play to shock us out of that complacency. If I said things like that as a lesbian feminist I'd be 'un-trendy' and 'a bit 70s' but it's fine if Daniel Keene says it. Anyway, in 1985 issue-based theatre and social justice were cutting edge. No-one in South Australia talks about social justice any more. The Liberals are in and social justice is out.

We began Vitalstatistix to produce work from a women's perspective for a general audience and to offer employment opportunities for women theatre workers. It's interesting that we focussed a number of productions on issues that women wanted us to write about. We didn't think about what we as artists wanted to express. We researched, set up improvisations, explored a mix of fantasy and reality, a variety of forms, women's humour, created characters based on our experiences. We also performed it. The issue was dieting and women's body image. *Weighing It Up* was a big hit. We were just doing the work: breaking new ground, performing in a huge variety of venues including theatres, making our dream of producing popular work from a feminist perspective a reality.

I was then, as I am now, Jewish. Yet the character I created in *Weighing It Up* was Greek. I find this interesting because eleven years ago, creating a Jewish character in a play and performing it, was not in my consciousness. Now, being a Jewish playwright is acceptable, interesting, multicultural, but then I didn't think so and neither did anyone else. I'm the daughter of two Austrian Jews who survived the Holocaust by escaping to Shanghai. My parents then fled during the Chinese Revolution to become refugees in 1950s Australia. I am tri-lingual. I speak Austrian, Yiddish and English fluently.

Next came *A Touchy Subject*. I find it interesting that in the 1990s it can sound quite cringey to say we wrote a play about sexual harassment but *A Touchy Subject* was incredibly popular, incredibly funny and effective. Ollie Black, Darrelyn Gunzberg and I wrote it and performed it for one and a half years. We then made a best-selling video resource kit which, as sexual harassment continues into the 1990s, is still selling.

I loved the process of improvising and writing, then performing.

As well as writing plays, I was well advanced with my main body of work—writing grant applications. I think it's an absolutely legitimate art form—I'm serious. I've looked at our archives and I estimate I've written at least 250 funding applications. I've poured my heart and soul into them. I've translated my visions and dreams and those of other women theatre workers into brief descriptions, synopses, summaries of background, process, innovative aspects, value of project to art form, value to Australian society, long term benefits, multicultural aspects, community, literary merit, style and content. Sometimes I've written five to eight applications for one project to vastly differing funding bodies, trusts and government departments. Vitalstatistix has pioneered in seeking non-arts funding for arts activities—my success rate was high.

So, one of my stars is for writing grant applications: it's the one that is metal with no star since this strand of my writing is so under-acknowledged, even by me.

I wrote *Home Sweet Home* in 1987 with Teresa Crea of Doppio Teatro. We were two artistic directors of theatre companies and our writing time had to be squeezed in between the demands of our other work but my yearning to work with women of non-English speaking background was nourished by the process. These were times when in small companies, development and writing times were short. Shows were written and produced in less than a year. The pressure was too much, too often. The work was good but we worked too hard. This was before I knew what the word 'dramaturg' meant.

I've had four of what one calls 'breakdowns' or episodes of mental illness in my life and I had one during one of the seasons of our cabaret show, *The Fabulous Apron Fashion Parade*. Roxxy and Ollie had to push me on stage. I could have been funnier if I wasn't so depressed. People who knew how funny I *could* be, noticed. It was hard on everyone, nevertheless the show was very popular. We did it in Sydney at The Performance Space. Intellectuals liked it. I was relieved. We performed it in the lounge car of a train going across the Nullarbor and in Perth.

By now, I had become the full-time Artistic Director. Vitalstatistix was producing the work of a wide variety of women playwrights. I think my insight as writer, performer and artist have made me a good artistic director although my version is more producer as I don't direct plays. As well as grant applications, I wrote publicity copy for all our shows with the publicists, dreamed up by-lines with writers, wrote program notes, press releases—this requires skill and is another aspect of my continual writing.

I also began to creatively develop *The Gay Divorcee*, born out of my real life trauma— the experience of a relationship ending—at the time I thought it was ending, but it wasn't, just changing. For a time, I was incapacitated. It triggered all sorts of emotions—grief and sadness and the others: hatred, jealousy, envy, the desire for revenge, plus I couldn't work. I could, however, write down my thoughts. After a while, a friend suggested that this would make a great play. I registered this and in the midst of it all, wrote a grant application.

I began to read about divorce and separation from all perspectives—straight, gay and lesbian. I undertook a survey of sex in long-term relationships. I continued to do my own therapy and began to work with Rosalba Clemente on developing a script. After a breakdown there can be a time of enormous creativity, clarity and inspiration. I worked collaboratively with the designer Cath Cantlon, dramaturg Tobsha Learner and the director Rosalba Clemente with input from Roxxy Bent. The process took one and a half years and the show, which I performed solo, was a great success. I wanted to change the gaze for a popular audience so they could gain insights and be entertained by writing from a lesbian experience. I wanted them to relate to and compare it with their own experience. *The Gay Divorcee* had sell-out seasons in both Adelaide and Sydney. In the process I came out publicly as a lesbian. This surprised fewer people than I'd thought. I found it harder to come out as a Jew, which is also a big part of the play.

So I was a writer of plays again. And a performer again. Apart from all the hard work and worry of being performer and producer as well, I loved being in this reality, not only facilitating the process for others, but for me too. I love the collaborative process. I work best in this way. The many years of working inclusively and with diverse groups of artists and communities means I am good at working out positive processes. I must say I still underestimate how long creativity takes and often Rosalba and Cath were frustrated by my being both artist and producer. I knew the cost of everything, worried about the publicity and every night counted the audience, working out how many concessions and full-prices—all from the giant clamshell I sat in at the beginning of each show.

In between seasons of *The Gay Divorcee*, I was back at the office and Vitalstatistix was changing. Ollie left, then Roxxy. We had initiated a management and company review to coincide with our tenth year in 1994 and began to assess our work and direction. We had a big dinner to honour the work and the women we'd worked with. We asked for feedback on the company past and present and whether the company had a role in the next decade. The answer was an overwhelming yes! There was as much need for a company producing women's work in 1994 as there had been in 1984—in many ways, more. From the writers, actors, directors we'd worked with we heard there were still hardly any women's plays being produced on mainstages, still fewer opportunities for women directors, designers, actors, and that in some ways, things had got worse. Feminism was not 'in'. We had entered the era of 'post-feminism', the media told us!

Meanwhile, women from all over Australia told us they loved working with us as we paid well and on time, were well organised, open, unpretentious and put artists first. I was flattered and pleased. Women in the industry acknowledged us as employers, visionaries, nurturers, skilled organisers and professionals who crossed boundaries and took risks.

In 1994, we were notified that we would not receive annual funding from the Performing Arts Board of the Australia Council for 1995. There had been no written or clear verbal communication that the PAB were having any problems with our work. The news was devastating. We were halfway through our self-initiated review and no-one had said our being funded depended on finishing the review before the Drama Panel of the PAB met.

I went through a gamut of emotions—shock, anger, sorrow and a sense that an enormous injustice had been done; that we who valued clear communication so highly had not been given this by a funding body. Delegates representing Vitalstatistix went to see the PAB. It was all dealt with professionally. Our de-funding was reported badly and inaccurately in the Adelaide press. Some people in the industry stopped talking to me. I was no longer in, we were out. I felt we'd failed, yet no-one had told us we were doing anything wrong. We'd thought 1994 was a fantastically successful year—all our other funding bodies thought so. I couldn't go to opening nights. Either people said nothing, or spoke to me in hushed tones like someone had died.

We examined ourselves, our work, doubted enormously, did everything well on a professional level and went without the $90,000. Vitalstatistix produced a program that was diverse, exciting and developmental and we chose not to do a show in 1995 as, on principle, it was silly to do so.

Cosmically, in the biggest picture, it was our destiny, our time to deal with what is perceived as a kind of disgrace. It's all fine. I've grown from it and I won't even ask the PAB to fund my next play. I love it that, personally, I don't want those dollars. Vitalstatistix re-applied but not for my new work. I can now go to opening nights again. So my blue star represents not being annually funded by the PAB. It's blue, as it was, in the end, a spiritual development.

So we continued with our review and changed Vitalstatistix totally. Not in response to the PAB but because it took a year to complete the review. We now have an all female Board which includes a representative from Vitalstatistix' Technical and Design Advisory Committee. I'm on it, so is Rosalba Clemente. In 1996 Vitalstatistix will become a national production house for women's work. We will have a yearly call for projects initiated by women artists of all kinds. We'll then choose three to produce for the year. We won't have an Artistic Director but an Executive Director instead and the project initiators will form an Artistic Forum to support each other's work. Our projects for next year are a show about Indigenous people and tourism by Eva Johnson and Catherine Fitzgerald, a play on breasts and breast cancer by Pat Rix and Kate O'Brien, my new play, *Wanted* and the creative development of Andrea Lemon's new play on women in rodeo. I won't work at Vitalstatistix after December. I'll be a freelance artist—this is a good thing.

In 1996 Vitalstatistix enters a new era. The evolution has been wonderful, hard, frustrating and has had input from many, many theatre workers, feminists and friends. This big star is for my work at Vitalstatistix over eleven years and for the company in the future. May she shine brightly.

I am writing again. My new project, *Wanted,* is eighteen months old and creatively developing. Once again, it's about Gretel, the character from *The Gay Divorcee.* She's now the head of an ethical feminist investment business, Fem Future. Her girlfriend Rita is a leading architect who has transformed the suburb in which Fem Future is based. Fem Future mentors young women and assists them in their studies—one such bright young woman is Virginia Swift. Gretel has just been named business woman of the year, she's respected, a workaholic and a bit too serious—then she discovers she's being defrauded by Faith Armstrong, her financial manager. She goes to Virginia's office to talk about what she's found and finds Virginia and Rita fucking on the desk—too much betrayal on all levels. Gretel gets a gun and shoots them, escapes by car and drives to the desert. She is *Wanted*. In the desert she goes wild, meets various beings including her dead father, Lilith, the Shekinah, Tantric sex goddesses and finally, a very attractive young reporter ...

Wanted's themes include feminism in the 70s and 90s, betrayal by women, spiritual workaholism, sex and the meaning of life. I'm working with Rosalba Clemente, Kerry Dwyer and Cath Cantlon on this one. Again, the play is semi-autobiographical although I didn't *actually* shoot anyone. The desert is the emptiness, the place of aloneness where the Jews wandered for forty years, where miracles happen and people die. It's a place of mystery and silence. I chose Kerry Dwyer because both Rosalba and I knew she could draw visions out of people, someone with great understanding of the many worlds, realities that can be explored. We went through the process Sue Ingleton described earlier—breathing, dancing, connecting; we spoke and saw beings in the desert, talked with them—the Shekinah, Lilith, an eagle, my father who is dead, and more.

We drew, we danced, talked, were amazed and then I went away to write. We were very careful to acknowledge that this was a collaboration, that the material was developed by us all.

I love research. For *Wanted* I've explored the meaning of life and Jewish spirituality which is so rich. I have been in a Jewish lesbian group in Adelaide for six years. I recently went to New York, to the 14th International Conference of Lesbian and Gay Jews. There were over 600 of us from over 20 countries. Then I went to a Jewish spiritual renewal retreat in the Catskills for a week and learned from a visionary rabbi in a community inclusive of gays and lesbians—it was truly wonderful.

I plan to work in New York next year. I have always longed for a connection with a world beyond the mundane and I am beginning to have one. I am not so hurt by injustice. I am and always will be an activist, an outsider, an agitator, but I am not so disappointed by people any more. I'm so relieved. Death has also been in my life, and I joined a synagogue. My therapist said everyone needs to belong to an organisation which has a spiritual base, so I went to a synagogue. I thought, oh no, now I'm a middle-aged woman I'm turning to religion! I've found the experience very enriching. Amazingly, I told the rabbi I was a lesbian and I spoke at a conference they ran. Now I've got a job writing a play about Jewish divorce for the Sisterhood of the Adelaide Progressive Synagogue, I can't seem to get away from the theme.

I am also involved in tantric sex. I just produced the Adelaide workshop by the tantric sex teacher, Barbara Carrellas. She's Annie Sprinkle and Penny Arcade's agent. It's marvellous. It's possible to have sex with the earth, the sky, the sea—I find these partners a lot more reliable than humans.

All of these things seem to be having a good effect on me personally and I hope on my writing.

So the last star, the small green and blue one, is for writing and the future—growth, and it's a chunky star with a bit of pink.

These ten years have been a long journey for me. I look forward to a further decade, more inspiration, joy, celebration, fame and fortune for me, for Vitalstatistix and for all of us.

PS Monday 16:10:96

This paper was very positively received by all at *Playing With Time*.
When I got back to Adelaide, Vitalstatistix was notified that
it had again not been granted annual funding by the Performing Arts Board.
This time we appealed and won.
The application will now be reconsidered in early March.
I feel fine about public places and opening nights.
I will now leave Vitalstatistix at the end of March.

02:45 PM

CATHY CRAIGIE AND MAY-BRIT AKERHOLT AT THE TABLE.
TIMEKEEPER SALLY RICHARDSON COUNTS COINS.

22   ▷ 22A   23

22   ▷ 22A   23

voices

cathy craigie

INTRODUCTION

Since 1993 the Australian National Playwrights Conference has developed nine Aboriginal & Torres Strait Islander plays by eight playwrights—four female and four male. The Conference forums have debated how we can overcome the expectations of theatre companies and audiences that writing should conform to European principles of drama which have informed our theatre for so long.

Mudrooroo in *Writing from the Fringe* argues that "Aboriginal dramatists are schizophrenic in that they must seek to please both non-Aboriginal and Aboriginal audiences. It is impossible for them to avoid this if they seek to have their works performed in the conventional theatre with its white middle class audience."

May-Brit Akerholt

THE TAPED VOICES OF SOME ABORIGINAL WOMEN.

Voices, Voices.....If I hear another "Wherefore art thou Romeo", I think I'll SSCREEAMM!

What the hell are they talking about?

"And the native women with their breasts exposed went on walkabout carrying their little piccaninnies."

I looked at myself. I was dressed in Levi jeans and a cut off T-shirt. My breasts weren't showing.

"You don't look like an Aborigine."

"You don't speak like an Aborigine."

"Are you full?"

What am I? A pint of milk? Caramel of course.

These stereotypical images of my people have been portrayed across stage and screen, in books and emblazoned on every newspaper and magazine in Australia. We don't have a life, we just march in protests, get drunk, resist any do-gooder white person and we definitely don't want to mix.

So say the non-Indigenous. The first peoples of this nation see it all so differently. We love, we laugh, we play—even tennis sometimes, we watch films, we like good food, we read newspapers ... Sound familiar? Yes, we seem to do the same things as everyone else out there.

Certainly there are things that are unique to Indigenous people. We have a wicked sense of humour, we love mixing with our own people, we love to eat bush foods, we are passionate about our lives, we are very emotional, love our land ...

So why don't we see this being reflected in the arts in Australia? Oh, I forgot, We are just 2% of the population—just a minority in the multicultural melting pot. Not important enough to warrant any effort or exposure. No, we are just the people whose land you're now all sitting on and whose land was stolen by your ancestors and continues to be stolen by your generation.

But no, every now and then we do see Aboriginal theatre, it creeps in and fades away just as quickly ... like in the year of the Bicentennial, 1988 or the Year of Indigenous People. Funny how Australians have this unnerving sense of guilt they are trying so hard to "reconcile". But at the same time they never admit what they are guilty of.

Guilty of cultural genocide, I say, both physically and psychologically. Look at the track record of the majority of theatre groups in this country. Throw an Aboriginal play in here, just this one off thing, keep up the multicultural component for the funding bodies, but nothing else for years. We did our bit. That will do. Did you know that the Sydney Theatre Company has never put on a full season of an Indigenous play? How many others are there, if one of Australia's most prestigious companies can't do it?

It really boils down to attitudes and money. Most companies never include in their yearly program the possibility of Koori theatre, they wipe it off as community theatre, (isn't that what all theatre is anyway?) or they do not have the funding and it stops there. Sometimes they will put a submission in to some Aboriginal and Torres Strait Islander funding body and ATSI funding goes outside again. Also there is the old attitude that European-based theatre is best. No acknowledgment of a people whose lives and culture were steeped in thousands of years of theatre. And not just theatre for stage, for the elite, but real theatre, theatre for the people.

It is for this reason that I decided to write—to give another insight, to take us out of the past and put us into the present. My writing is about Kooris today. For so long, nothing Aboriginal was accepted in the Australian arts scene without it being based in the past. That way you do not have to confront the present. "I'm not guilty of anything; that all happened in the past" is the usual catchcry. I write because I want to confront. I use language that is ours, I use the rhythms and the patterns of English as we speak it amongst ourselves. I use our own words and phrases. I present images that are today— frightening images of what colonisation has done. I write in the hope that our people will see the wider picture—what is happening to us. My plays are emotional, they are steeped in Koori tradition, they draw on the past to present the future. *Murri Love*, for example, follows the relationship and strength of two Indigenous women in the face of domestic violence.

Many times my words go over the head of the non-Kooris in the audience but then I think back to my own experience. Try and work it out, it gives you a better insight! A richer experience, a better understanding.

As Paul Galloway reviewing my play *Murri Love* said:

I didn't get some of the jokes in Murri Love, *they went right over my head landing right behind me where the Murri audience sat and laughed. It was an unsettling experience. Most theatre panders to the likes of me—Anglo Saxon. I had come to take it for granted. I can watch, say,* Kafka Dances, *about a neurotic Jewish writer living in the Bohemia of the late Austrian Empire and feel right at home. Despite the surface exotica, it speaks my language, European, literate, indeed literary and replete with familiar symbols and references. But a culture which thrives not eight kilometres from where I live, had me flummoxed. While the Murris roared, I felt as if I had been dropped off in Alpha Centauri.*

Murri Love was produced in1995 by Brisbane's Kooemba Jdarra.

A few years earlier, Belvoir Street Theatre did a production of this same play but then it was called *Koori Love*. I remember cringing on opening night. How I had pictured this work was not what was up on stage. It was my first play and the director's too. We both were too inexperienced to really do what we wanted. There is a theory that the oppressed often mimic their oppressors and this was definitely true of early Aboriginal theatre. Yes, the subjects were Aboriginal but the shape, the structure, even the language was not ours. I have vivid memories of other Koori plays having the actors speaking broken English instead of Aboriginal English. And there is a big difference. Aboriginal English is rhythmic, has different sounds, uses different meanings for words. It is the language used by most Aboriginal people who have been bought up in an Aboriginal environment.

My play *Koori Love* back then was reviewed as "raw", not much to write home about. I agree it was raw but I do strongly believe that the reviewers too, just like the reviewer of *Murri Love*, had been totally used to Eurocentric theatre.

When Kooemba Jdarra, the Indigenous theatre company in Brisbane, asked me to submit *Koori Love* I did so with not much confidence in the play. But the director, Wesley Enoch is a Murri himself. He was excited and believed that we could do something with it. After three weeks of working with an all Murri cast, *Murri Love* was born and I knew that I could now walk away from this play and move on. Even the actors who had quite a lot of experience between them thought that this was one of the best plays they had acted in. The audience reacted in the same way.

It is for this response that I write. I do not feel comfortable with the label 'writer'. I am an Aboriginal person who uses writing as a tool for raising awareness of Indigenous issues, people and lifestyles. An Aboriginal writer can't really write in isolation. She/he has a responsibility to the community. What we write is reflected in our community. There is one theme that runs through the writing of all Aboriginal writers: we always discuss our families and community. I can't think of any story written by an Aboriginal person that doesn't bring this sense of family and community in. We do not see ourselves as being on our own. I think that it is this sense of being that makes our work different from other writers in Australia. It is the core of our stories.

And we have a lot of stories to tell. Europeans have told their stories over and over. There really is nothing new. Some European writers even have to appropriate other cultures. But for Indigenous people there are thousands of stories within their community just waiting to be told. In the past, we have not been allowed to tell our stories but as this changes, the truth of Australia is beginning to unfold. I just hope that I can be part of this unfolding.

*The idea of the 'voice'—who speaks, who controls discourse, who is heard—
has important implications for the Australian context.
If we are to speak of cultural identities it is necessary to know how they are articulated,
not just what is being said.*

Patrick Fuery
Representations, Discourse and Desire
(Longman Cheshire)

20   KODAK 5053 TMY   21   KOD

20   KODAK 5053 TMY   21   KOD

' ‡ '

amanda stewart

A NOTE ON THE PERFORMANCE

‡ is a semantically engendered piece. I composed a text in which the word order was set but the performance of these words was to be spontaneously manipulated by the voice according to specific oral modes of articulation. I recorded the first performance onto the left channel and then recorded a second text on the right channel which overhears, comments on and interjects over the first. The third and fourth layers are stereo vocal improvisations which make occasional comments.

The texts use a diversity of references and constructions from schizoid operatic personal pronouns like sh e it, to mercurial tirades, fractured English, phonemes, calls, statements, outbursts, stutters, mouth sounds, 'concrete nouns', parallel speech ... so that modes of listening are constant, switching between different fields of shape and suggestion.

The title of the piece, ‡ (not equal), refers to its construction and to ideas suggested by the two texts. On one level, the piece explores a lack of equivalence between graphic and aural inscription (ie modes of memory).

In ‡, the four layers were recorded on six tracks on a multi-track recorder as consecutive, 'live' improvisations to tape. They were then mixed to two track without editing or processing.

EXCERPT FROM ‡

i
   was an individual
   and an attempt
   at generalisation.

     i
i   you
 was a
  despite what ^i says

  object of too
  is relation through

      i
  it 'n' self 'n' you ishly

  pluralistic lipsurface
  on the face of things   things

  holes full of
     bright blue absence
  why is a straight line ?
     a plurality of thes
  and i the father the one
     the subject
  icons of spatials

i   it exchanged.

    ing
     west   itself
  culture found its

absent in nature therely so
then absent within itself
      him

as a wild ^psych unconscious ^tech

phenomenon
of things

use use use   mad owing

yes yes yes
artifacts in space

geometries of cultured noise'

145

34 KODAK 5053 TMY 35 KOI

34 KODAK 5053 TMY 35 KOI

the lover and the beloved

alana valentine

TAPE: *CARSON McCULLERS*

First of all, love is a joint experience between two persons—but the fact that it is a joint experience does not mean that it is a similar experience to the two people involved. There are the lover and the beloved, but these two come from different countries. Often the beloved is only the stimulus for the stored-up love which has lain quiet within the lover for a long time hitherto. And somehow every lover knows this. He feels in his soul that his love is a solitary thing. He comes to know a new, strange loneliness and it is this knowledge which makes him suffer. So there is only one thing for the lover to do. He must house his love within himself as best he can. Let it be added here that this lover about whom we speak need not necessarily be a young man saving for a wedding ring— this lover can be man, woman, child, or indeed any human creature on this earth ...

from The Ballad of the Sad Cafe, *Penguin Books*
(first published in Great Britain by the Cresset Press, 1953)

NOTE: THE TAPED EXCERPT HAS BEEN EDITED HERE

That was a recording of Carson McCullers reading from *The Ballad of the Sad Cafe*. It was a gift to me from Rebecca Holderness, the director of my play *Southern Belle*, and it was part of the research she did to direct a reading of the play at New Dramatists in New York earlier this year.

I travelled to New York as the recipient of the 1994 ANPC/New Dramatists Award. The award is administered by the ANPC who send five scripts to New York and New Dramatists, purportedly the oldest playwrighting development agency in that city, choose the writer they want to invite to New York to take part in two readings of their work, theatre going and general literary and performance hobnobbing. The Americans call the award the Sumner Locke Elliott Award after the Australian writer who lived most of his life in the USA. When he died he left New Dramatists all his money and also any monies deriving from the sale of the rights to his works subsequent to his death. But to return to Carson McCullers...

The cassette was used in the reading to help the actors perform with a specifically Georgian accent rather than a Southern approximation. You've all heard that one, the Southern accent that despite the valiant attempts of sincerely dedicated actors,

ranges from Louisiana to Carolina and ricochets around Mississippi before settling into
something twangily close to Birmingham in Alabama. New Dramatists actually arranged
for a Georgian speech consultant, Eliza Hurt Lloyd to work with me on the script. It was
the rarest of gifts to work with someone who so intricately understood the nuances and
subtleties of Southern speech. I was gratified by her comments that the thematic thrust
of the script was correct, for instance, the representation of the North/South rivalry and
the experience Southerners have of being colonised by the North.

When I went to the States my stated aim was to look at the cadences and rhythms of
the speech and test how right I had got them and gratefully again, little of this changed.
What did change were particularly colloquialisms. For instance, I had a doorman in the
play who 'guards' the prestigious Southern Kennedy Club into which Carson is never
allowed, referring to African-Americans as 'blacks'. Eliza took me through the various
indications of status that were afforded at that time to the terms 'negroes', 'negras' and
'niggers'. 'Negroes' was a very formal form of address, used as a mark of respect. 'Nigger'
was completely derogatory and 'negra' is somewhere in between, ie still subordinate but
without an overtly hostile tone.

But this year, during my play reading, was not the first time I had heard Carson McCullers'
voice. And that's the reason I wanted to talk about this play today, as we celebrate ten
years of women's writing through Playworks. Because when I look back over the last
ten years of my life I find that they are distinctly coloured by my literary love affair with
Carson McCullers—an affair in which I have very much been the lover trying to strip bare
the heart of my beloved, as Carson so eloquently and unforgettably described in that
opening reading we heard.

Not that I have been writing the play for ten years. And even if I had, I probably
shouldn't admit to it. I vividly remember the British playwright Louise Page, author of
Salonika among other works advising me: "Always say you've been working on something
for about a year. That way it sounds like you've got a commitment to it without being
obsessive. Anything over a year and they'll think oh, my God, it's art!" But I have been
thinking about the play on and off for all that time, so as a part of this ten year celebration
I wanted to pose myself the question that has been asked of me so many times since I
began writing this play and having it read: Why would an Australian woman want to write
a play about a dead Southern American writer of the 1940s and 50s?

I first heard Carson McCullers reading from her own work when I travelled to the USA
to research the play in 1987. That trip was actually something of a Carson McCullers
pilgrimage which took me from her home town in Columbus, Georgia to her final resting
place in Nyack, New York State. In Columbus I was entertained by the President of the
Friends of Carson McCullers Society, Miss Margaret Sullivan whose prize possession was

a small hymn book in which the young and rebellious Carson had scrawled her name. She also took me to Carson's childhood home and put me in contact with her biographer Dr. Virginia Spencer Carr with whom I have had several correspondences. She also introduced me to Dr. Mary Mercer, Carson's psychiatrist for the last twenty years of her life and the woman to whom she dedicated her last book, *Clock Without Hands*.

I visited the library in Columbus where there was a small glass cabinet displaying some photos of Mrs. McCullers and where the librarian, when questioned, couldn't help but remind me that Carson was more than a little odd. And it struck me, as had much of my experience of the Deep South, that what many of these writers were writing about—the small town, small minded hatred of difference, the racial bigotry, the poverty, the violence—were not simply preserved historical literary truths, but current reflections of the state of the Union. Carson McCullers was still frowned upon for her radical anti-racist politics, her ambiguous sexuality, rejected as an unworthy representative of her home town. Her birthplace had been torn down and made into a freeway while the birthplace of one of her Southern literary peers, William Faulkner, is preserved as a museum, his bust reproduced on postage stamps. At this point I can only quote from Carson herself who said, "I write better than Hemingway and God knows I have more to say than Faulkner."

The more I followed the life of this extraordinary writer the more its powerful contradictions spoke to me. I was hoping to see some of her manuscripts in the Columbus Library but she had refused to donate them. When they asked for them in 1958 it was still a segregated library where books from the 'white' section were trolleyed across to another library for use by the 'blacks' and 'coloureds'. I understand that all her manuscripts were instead purchased by the University of Texas in Austin (which I had visited earlier in my trip without knowing!) Some were in Nyack where she spent the last twenty years of her life before dying at the tragically young age of 50. Strangely enough, my own mother was later to die three days short of her fiftieth birthday. I'll look at some parallels with my own experience in a moment.

I went to the Nyack Library and listened to Carson read from her own work. I walked to the Nyack Cemetery, to the top of the hill where Carson is buried, overlooking the beautiful Hudson River. Her mother Marguerite is buried beside her. And if you have ever seen my play or know anything of Carson's life, you will know that she had a particularly vexed relationship with her mother (something I'm sure will be unfamiliar to most of us!) I sat next to Carson's grave and it was there, I think, that the seed of my play *Southern Belle* germinated.

I must admit that I was never asked in America why an Australian would want to write a play about Carson McCullers. I have frequently been asked it here, as though invalidating the appropriateness of my desire to write such a play can be used as a way of ignoring and diluting its dramatic conclusions. Ah yes, you say, but Americans think that the whole world is obsessed with them, even if it is with the mucky, now very fashionable South. I don't think that's the reason. I think that the Americans accepted that the experience of American Southerners might dangerously parallel the experience of some Australians.

Of course, many of us accept that as a writer you can write about anything. I suppose what I learned from this experience is what every biographer knows: that in writing about someone else you are, ultimately or partially writing about yourself; that you can use your creativity and your imagination to inhabit other skins but that, finally, the passion of the convictions in your work will come from the parallel truths of lived experience.

Several weeks ago I was interviewed about my work on Radio National by David Britton. He began the interview by asking me about my childhood and my desire to be a writer. I was completely thrown. I never talk about my childhood. I never write about it, or do therapy on it or even think very much about it. And yet, in considering the last ten years and this obsession with Carson McCullers and other Southern writers I realise how much South American writing speaks to me about my experience, in a way that is different from much Australian writing. These are stories in which the culture of poverty is so onerous as to appear vulgar and exaggerated. Stories where violence and fear of difference are inseparable, bludgeoning and unable to be examined in any useful or instructive manner. Ruth Park and Christina Stead, Dorothy Hewett and Katherine Thomson speak of this culture in Australia but in different ways I think from the Gothic horror of the Southern Americans.

In her poem *When we are Lost,* Carson describes time as "an endless idiot" who "runs screaming round the world". I'd like to suggest that women's experience in time also runs screaming around the world and that in the context of Playworks' theme I'd like to see the next ten years in Australian writing helping us to play also with the context so that we can use fiction to mine the complexities of our experience and deepen these resonances.

In New York, much was made of parallel experiences of colonisation of Australia and the South. As many questions were raised about the colonisation of Northern American culture in Australia as the invasion of the British. But more was made of my perspective as the outsider who could write about Carson McCullers' life unencumbered by the axe-grinding of a defensive Southerner or cynical Northerner.

And I was, I think, productively confronted with my own questions about how my perspective might be dated or prejudicial or simplistic. I was answered with the conviction that all writing is subjectively personal and biographical writing is totally fictional. I was forced, in this American context, to concentrate on the indelible and universal resonances of Carson McCullers' conclusion that her home town was never going to accept her.

And so, finally, the enthusiasm of my play's reception in New York was the very thing which liberated me from Carson's conclusion. It allowed me to see that her alienation was most painfully a trap, an edifice which she eventually could not escape, a position which came to define her identity. And I returned to Australia with a strong desire to move on, knowing that this was her story, not mine; that I wanted to write the stories of people at other places in the social spectrum in this country; I wanted to test the skins of other men and women and explore their discoveries.

03:30 PM ▬▬▬▬▬▬▬▬▬▬ interruption

MAY-BRIT AKERHOLT INTERRUPTS WITH A SUMMING UP

Cathy Craigie's arguments—and a lot of the talks I've heard over this conference— reminded me for some strange reason about the Icelandic Sagas—they tell of families, heroic and ordinary women and men, their battles for honour, love, power, goods. Influenced by other European literature (heroic epics from France and Germany) they are unique in their form with highly developed and complex characterisation, vivid and passionate dialogue, very dramatic and theatrical. The important thing is that they were written in an environment with a strong sense of cultural importance. They were telling their stories and in doing that, mythologising their lives.

A story is something true because a person, somewhere, at some time, lived it. But a myth is a story that is more than true because it is lived by all of us, at some level. It is the story beneath the story.

We need to mythologise our lives so our stories can live in all of us.

Nearly all plays have characters and stories we are familiar with, or at least recognise certain aspects of. But the secret of a good play lies in its difference from all other plays, in the individual voice of the playwright, the specific way the writer mythologises a life, tells its story, gives it a unique perspective. Cathy Craigie and Alana Valentine—a lot of women—write from a passion for their subjects, rather than wondering which theatre company will produce it or how many characters they can get away with. They really use their own voices. So their characters become not just fictional, but idiosyncratic: genuine because the writers have given them their own passions, emotions and idiosyncrasies.

So, ten years of research, obsession, visits, tangible facts, Carson McCullers' own voice and finally, the enthusiastic reception for her play in New York, liberated Alana from the conclusion her heroine had come to, to a reality that Carson McCullers' alienation was a position that came to define her identity. And that realisation, and Cathy's realisation that her writing could change the stereotypical images Kooris, all Aborigines live and labour under, lead to a sort of liberation and experience for the playwrights which are conveyed to their audiences. They have not only told their stories, they have mythologised them, so they can live forever.

LANGUAGE

Amanda Stewart starts with a set word order—a conventional structure—then she uses a mixture of technology, her own imagination, improvisation, and feeds it all into a kind of spontaneous manipulation of words, structures, tracks, to provide layers of language and meaning. She creates a new text, a different imagination in which rhythms, tone and patterns form a unique voice. Alana Valentine's quest is also for a language that can capture the cadences and rhythms of her character's speech. Cathy Craigie's quest is similar: an effort to create a theatrical language from the rhythms and speech patterns in the English that Indigenous people use among themselves. In doing this, their plays achieve an authority and genuineness in tone and dialogue which make them work as drama. The language these writers create for their characters liberates them and gives them dignity and purpose: it also creates new dimensions of theatrical language, ie their language has been given dignity by becoming a stage language. It's our language. It's our stage language which is becoming increasingly imaginative and eloquent in the way it speaks to us.

What is an Australian stage language? It isn't the use of Aussie slang or expressions: it's a language written by us, performed by us for our audiences, whether the play is set in urban or suburban Australia, a country town, the South of USA: whether it's a new Australian work or a translation for our stage. Australian theatre is made up of more than Australian drama. Cultural diversity includes an appropiation of works written in other languages and making them part of our repertoire. Since English translators started to take themselves seriously after the first World War (some of them women) a terrible crop of earnest translations have dominated the market on the English-speaking stage. We used to stage Chekhov set in English rose-gardens with starched nannies: Ibsen's characters became male stereotypical fumbling fools who had wonderfully strong women inexplicably falling in love with them. We have come a long way, not only by writing new versions for our productions but also by staging and interpreting the classics in light of ourselves and our lives. And just as it's the playwright's unique voice which infuses the characters with their unique voices, their passions and emotions, it's the translator's individual and distinct style and voice which will make the new version live and breathe in its new country with its peculiar character, relevant to its society and audience, becoming part of its literature and theatrical repertoire.

The best plays written by Australian playwrights today, including those on our panel, and works by Beatrix Christian, Katherine Thomson, Dorothy Hewett, Alma de Groen, Suzanne Spunner—and many male writers—are works that have the qualities which for me make them 'classic': works that prey on us, that engage the mind and the heart so that there is no real distinction between the way we react intellectually and emotionally, even spiritually, when we watch them in the theatre. It's time our theatre companies started to feed us a good and varied diet which satisfies the head as well as the stomach, or audiences will start thinking that hamburger is real gourmet food.

04:20 PM

15:10:1995

A WEAVING OF WORDS AS JENNIFER COMPTON, MELISSA REEVES AND MARY HUTCHISON INTERRUPT EACH OTHER CONVERSATIONALLY, COMPARING DECADES.

THE TIMEKEEPER, FRANCESCA SMITH, PEELS AND PARES APPLES.

30   KODAK 5053 TMY   31   KOD

30   KODAK 5053 TMY   31   KOD

time passes

jennifer compton

My text for today is from an American director talking about Uncle Vanya—*Yeliana shouldn't play the characters' perceptions of her.*

It's cold out here in my Willow Cabin in the middle of the vegetable garden with a fine view of the compost heaps and the willows planted in the outflow from the septic tank—because I smashed a window pane last month. I had locked myself out and became desperate to get back in to write the play that I knew was in there. It was harder to smash a pane of glass than I would have thought. I had to give it three good ones.

What a lot of money and patience has been expended on me since I arrived in Australia in 1971 so I can type *The End* in my Willow Cabin in July 1995 and stand up and say—Now, at last, I know how to write a play. How many good friends have watched me standing on the end of the pier ripping up my best chances and throwing them away. But you're not ready until you're ready. Some of them lost patience. Some of them died.

One of them said—Oh my God, Jennifer. Don't have a baby. You'll never write another word.

So 1985 finds me with a week-old daughter, a two year old son and post natal depression. I didn't know it was depression because it manifested itself as anxiety. One of the symptoms was that I couldn't tell anyone about it.

Backtrack backtrack. In 1984 when I was pregnant with my daughter, the then dramaturg of the Sydney Theatre Company invited twenty women writers to submit a one act play. My husband hired a nanny and I got to work. I submitted the play and waited and waited. Getting huger and huger. In November I read in the *Herald* the names of the four plays that had been picked. I rang up and asked for my play to be sent back. It came back with the reassuring comment from the then dramaturg that he was sure the play would have a life of its own.

I think I can see now that that rejection was a triggering factor. I had and have all sorts of ways of dealing with rejection but back then one of the ways I dealt with it was to say to myself—I'm being rejected because I'm a woman. It was the first time I had lost in an all woman race.

But I gritted my teeth and sent the play out and about. Out and about. Out and about. "It's not dramatic." "It won't work." "Funny! It's not funny."

I had sent it to everybody twice over and well and truly given up on it. But poverty compelled me to cut my losses and I wrote a radio version. The readers' reports were so bad I wasn't allowed to see them. One director refused to direct it. One director indicated her distaste for the play. Finally, a good friend to me directed it and I was happy with the production. But Katharine Brisbane asked me which version I preferred and in a very small voice I admitted—the first one.

Fast forward fast forward. In 1993 Sue Hill at Belvoir Street Theatre idly asked me if I had a one act play. I sent her the radio version and included the scorned stage version just to show her it had originally been a stage play. On the first day of rehearsal I suddenly realised that the director wanted to do the stage version. I screamed with fright.

And it did work. And it was funny. I was right.

But that was in 1993. I wrote it in 1984. Patience. Patience.

So. 1985. I emerged from post play rejection depression and considered my situation. I decided I had had enough. Enough of slaving my guts out. Enough of watching my work disappear into the void. I had had enough of being on the receiving end of bad manners and bad faith. I had had enough of waiting in line to be passed over. That was what it felt like. I felt very angry and very hurt. I had thought of myself as a writer for a very long time. I had sold two poems when I was 14 for five pounds seven and six per insertion. It's my working class background. If they pay you for it, then that's what you are.

I was lying in bed one afternoon among the litter of sleeping children. The wardrobe door was ajar. I could see the sleeve of my coat. I thought—being a writer is like putting on a coat. And if you can put it on you can take it off. I took the coat off. I was no longer a writer.

I set about finding out how the people who are not writers live. Why do they get up in the morning? How do they get through the day? What sends them to sleep at night?

It makes me smile to think of myself setting off with one in the stroller and one on my hip to research real people. It's such a writers' thing to do.

Playworks appears in my life.

A friend rang me up—Jennifer, you know that play you were writing in 1980 when we met in Christchurch, the play that opens with the heroine replacing a pane of glass in her window, have you nearly finished it because there's this ad in the paper for women's plays to workshop?

My days were full of children and housework so I started writing at night. My daughter could sense when the work started to take me over. I couldn't hear her crying out in my room but I could hear my husband's footsteps across the kitchen floor and the window being thrown up. "Jennifer, she's crying."

All The Time In The World was workshopped and showcased in 1987. I had only subliminally noticed that it was Playworks *Women* Writers Workshop. For some reason I had never considered sending a play to the Australian National Playwrights Conference.

Maybe it was because the registration fee for Playworks was very cheap. Maybe it was just because someone had asked me to write a play. That I was feeble enough to stand around waiting to be asked to dance. But on the first day at the Randwick Literary Institute, Ros Horin asked for all the writers to gather. We gathered. And I'm looking from side to side and feeling uneasy and thinking—there's something really peculiar about these writers. And I twig. We're all the same size. In the past, in my previous incarnations as a TV writer, as a radio writer, as a poet, as a playwright, when two or three writers were called together, chances were they were all men—and me. And they always seemed to be such big men. I had to tilt my head back and look way way up and pitch my voice higher and try to get way way up there. So. A writer can be little. But her voice can be big.

Nothing has come of that play that was workshopped in 1987. You have all told me, over and over again—"It won't work." "It's not dramatic." Da de da de da de da de da. Some of you have even called it a fine piece of writing. You are all wrong. And I'm not repairing the smashed pane of glass in my window until you admit it.

Time passes. I'm on top of the children and I complain to Anna Volska that I'm feeling a bit sort of lonely and bored. Anna rings up Jo Fleming at Playworks and I am welcomed onto the committee. I begin to figure out how it works. I start to tune into what's going down. I feel safer and safer. I start to snap up chances. I'm offered script assessment work. I'm offered the opportunity to try my hand at dramaturgy. I am on the other side of the fence. Then I'm in the thick of things. I begin to make my own opportunities.

I'm ready for second chances. In 1994 Ros Horin invites me to submit a one act play for possible inclusion in Griffin's *Passion* season at The Stables Theatre. I have no faith in any happy outcome, I've been through all this before, but she is offering me money for a first draft. I write it. Then she is offering me money to write a second draft. I write it. Then she is accepting *Barefoot* for production. Oo er. I won't say it wasn't a bumpy ride— at the first read-through I suddenly realised I had made all sorts of cultural assumptions that the people who have to make the play work don't share. Error. Big mistake.

Meanwhile. Because a good friend to me had rigorously drilled me in the writing of grant applications, one of the most important genres a writer can get a handle on, I had finally pulled a grant to write a play from the Australia Council.

I sat down to write a first draft. Because of my happy experience working with Ros. I look into the future and see the steps you take when you sit down to write a play. I believe I can write a play. I believe it will be produced.

Time passes and time passes.

And here we are—it's 4:45 pm 15:10:95

sunday

04:45 PM

15:10:1995

20   KODAK 5053 TMY   21   KOD

20   KODAK 5053 TMY   21   KOD

the art of public speaking

mary hutchison

Lines words ... when are you going to write this play?
Lines
Dialogue
Words
Can we cut some of the words?
This bit needs a few words
We don't want to use words
Mary'll do the words

Language
Text
Poetry
When are you going to write this play?

I'm on a train, somewhere in Britain in the mid-1970s. I'm reading TS Eliot. I discover that poems are made, not of singly meaningful words, but images. This lesson seems to hold ...

It's earlier in the 1970s. I'm a drama student at Flinders University. I discover that I am not a performer. I also discover that the action of a play is expressed through the characters' words. The fascination I find in a textual analysis of the masters' characters' words is akin to the interest I take in the interaction of people around me; their intentions, the way they mask their intentions, play down, exaggerate—and how this all connects with wider worlds of social meaning. I study sociology instead of drama and in the early 80s start putting the two together. The lesson about the words of the characters does not seem to hold ...

The playwright who gives me hope in the 1980s is Caryl Churchill. The meaning of form starts to open up for me. I feel less harnessed to the masters' characters' words. She gives me hope because she does hard and subtle things, strange, complex things.

In the 1980s I also get a grip on the sociology of the theatre—the importance of developing and maintaining good working relationships with directors. In the wake of the Women and Theatre Conference I start seeking partnerships with women directors. Sometimes this works. Sometimes it doesn't. But the things I achieve with Camilla Blunden, Gail Kelly and Chris Johnson make me bold. I start writing dialogue so that it looks more like verse than naturalistic speech. I feel assured about the images I make with language. I work more successfully with layer and resonance.

But although I value and feel secured by the idea of a working relationship with a director and take real pleasure in the collaboration that takes place, I am still struggling towards some perfect point of authority, when I will have mastered the process, myself, the world enough to write a pure, transparent script that will be instantly performable. I am hooked on being a writer, an author. Although I am starting to manipulate form and image for myself and I have never forgotten another lesson from my Flinders days—that it is not the single frame but the juxtaposition of frames that makes meaning—I still have a simplistic individualistic notion of writing itself.

PERFORMANCE

In about 1983 I wrote a monologue called *The Art of Public Speaking*. It was about fear of speaking, lack of voice, and it was one of those occasions when I really let myself speak—contrary to all dictates I opened my mouth and let the words come out. I didn't care. It was published in Hale and Iremonger's *Angry Women* anthology. From the vantage point of now, I see it as a piece rather like the first thing I ever had published—in the school magazine—a weird, associative piece, oddly strong. Why, I ask myself, didn't I pursue this style that leaped from my 17 year old brow? Perhaps it's one of those astral phenomena that appears only at appointed moments in a lifetime.

I suppose one of the marvels of *The Art of Public Speaking* for me is that it still captures the undercurrents of a major aspect of my work—whether as a writer, teacher or social historian—my interest in voice.

You know those glasses of water they have on the conference table or when someone gives a speech? They always look like this water tastes. It must be so wonderful when you've been talking to all those people, or in front of cameras and then you just take a dignified pause and a sip of water. Raise the glass to your lips. But it's not a sip and it's not a gulp. The water just slides down your throat. Effortlessly. You don't have to make it go down. It wants to. And after this cool, clear, liquid experience you put the glass down and you face the audience and your words are clear, bell like. And singers. They gargle don't they?...

Wouldn't it be terrible if you were a singer and you gargled the wrong way—it might come out of your nose and you'd get that awful scraping feeling in your throat, you know that feeling when you're swimming and you think you're gulping in air, but you actually get water in with it and you try and cough it up, but some of it's already gone down your nose—too late. You nearly choke and then it's burning along your nasal passages, tearing away at the lining as it goes. And what if you were giving a terribly

*important speech and you took this pristine glass of water in your venerable hand and
raised it to your lips and snorted up the water, and there you were, coughing and
spluttering and drowning with the eyes of the world on you.*

from *The Art of Public Speaking* in Di Brown et al (eds) *Angry Women:
An Anthology of Australian Women's Writing* (Hale and Iremonger, NSW,1989)

VOICE

It's the voices we don't hear that interest me.
What is the framework that will enable them to be heard?
What may drown them out?

When I try to write about voice, I start to write about story.

Oral history has played a key role in my work as a social historian. In writing for the
theatre in the1980s I gravitated towards community theatre because of its interest in
individuals' renderings of their own experiences. In the late 80s I seized the opportunity
to work more directly with stories and voices through community writing and publishing
workshops. This form of writing work has been home to me for some time.

'The girl smiled'.
The girl smiles
says fuck
screams
refuses
steps out
purrs
flies away
swings shut
I am the girl.
I am the amazon who dances on the backs of turtles.
I am the efficient blue suited office worker who clips her words quietly and her nails loudly.
I am the briefcase holding my hand.
I am the oracle who knows where the foundation springs from but no-one will listen.
I'm not telling.
I am the radar who will find out.
I am the sister of the amazon who dances on turtles and she will protect me from the radar.

from *I am the amazon who dances on the backs of turtles*
Jena, Paris, Lisa, Margaret, Sue, Lyn. Research Workshop, June 1991.

That was put together by six members of Homefront Women's Writing Group, in a writing workshop. The exercise started with 'the girl smiled' and the object was to cross out each line and write a new one, changing the story, by action, subject, position. If it was theatre we'd call it improvisation.

Homefront Women's Writing Group started life as a group of ex-residents of a Canberra women's refuge who were interested in taking part in various activities, including writing. Over a period of three years, in which they acquired project funding, administrative support from the Incest Centre and then independent status as Homefront, they produced and distributed two publications, became readers/performers of their own work and began to lead workshops for other women.

Leading these workshops has been one of the most significant and formative aspects of my writing work. I developed a lasting connection with adult education and literacy work and found a much more satisfying way of working in a community environment than community theatre was promising at the time. Most importantly, in looking for the ways in which other people could say what they wanted to say in their own voices, in their own words, I had the chance to work with the shapes and forms of language. How not to tell an incest experience in the discourse of popular magazines, how not to tell it in PC feminist style, how to tell it so the subject is present, but not the object of voyeurism?

The girl smiles
says fuck
screams
refuses
steps out
purrs
flies away
swings shut
I am the girl.
I am the amazon who dances on the backs of turtles.

What happened to theatre?
At the same that I was travelling towards my death as an author I was working in puppet theatre. The relationship between objects and language is very different from that between actors and language. Naturalistic use of language in theatre became less and less interesting for me. I became more interested in the making of meaning through action, and integrating language into this as one might integrate music or lighting. But it wasn't until Peter Wilson took up the artistic directorship of Canberra's Company Skylark that I had an opportunity to really try this out—it feels pretty raw still, but hopeful.

It's only relatively recently as I discover that I've let theatre work go enough in order to be able to take it up again, that I've been able to see how my interest in writing for performance and what I've learned from it, has impacted on the other ways in which I've taken up writing work.

In my writing workshops I encourage people to work with what they have to say in their everyday speaking voices. I set up exercises which involve people listening to each other and writing down what others say, not in note form for content, but verbatim, for rhythm. I often work with large sheets of paper, writing down what people say, in the way they say it, so that everyone can see what's happening, and we can shape it together.

In working with people who do not want to write themselves I act as a scribe—a technique I developed in association with Annie Bolitho—and then, through reading back what I have taken down, invite them to further compose the work. In scribing like this I use line breaks that work with speech rhythms—the same approach I have taken to 'dialogue' in the past.

In retrospect I see that constructing a book where variation in tone may be heard and difference in perspective read, is not unlike making a play. What can sit next to what? What is the broad shape? What are the conventions and how are they established? Where is the space for the reader? Who are the characters? In *Hells Belles' Letters,* each writer had her own four pages which she designed herself in relation to what she had written.

I'm sure it works the other way too—that what I have learned about writing and story through community writing and publishing impacts on the way I approach theatre writing. In working on a piece about Katherine Susannah Prichard I felt that the most effective thing I could contribute was to contextualise or re-contextualise what she had written and said herself. The writing challenge was what the performance would say about Prichard and how to control and shape that by selection and placement. I wrote a kind of prologue to the piece in the style of one of Prichard's poems and in the end realised that even that wasn't necessary.

In the nineties my work as a writer is about form, context, rewriting, re/presentation. The Author has been quietly replaced by the pleasures of creating telling work with other people—sometimes people who bring considerable artistic experience in one form or another to the activity, sometimes people who simply have something to say and want to explore how to do that with resonance and texture.

WORKING AS A WRITER—CAREER MOVES

The area of writing and making that I most want to develop is that of handmade books. Working on a writing and sculpture project in 1990 at Revolve, the Recycling

Depot at Mugga Lane Tip in Canberra, I discovered not only found text (something you could say I've been working with ever since) but the potential for certain objects to become books. Of course every day in that environment was a performance.

Making changes—making tracks 1:10:90

On their first operations fighter pilots report the experience of not being able to see any enemy aircraft. They don't know how to focus in that great expanse. Gradually the sky becomes readable. On my first day at the Tip everything could have been anything. I didn't know what I was looking at. I just took some snaps for the record ... I tried hard to keep track, to name and place.

Today I saw five chairs that I'm sure the British used in Africa circa the turn of the century. Hinged seats and hinged arms—they fold up perfectly. White canvas and solid, bevelled and varnished. A representation or recollection of cedar or blackwood. Sylvia bought them for her mud brick house in the Warrumbungles. Margaret said she would borrow one when she goes into the field.

In fact the story of the Chairs became the subject of another book, chronicled through letters between Margaret, Sylvia and myself.

Today I also saw an ancient cement mixer with a gear lever, three big black letters— RDO—they looked heavy but were quite light—a book documenting an exhibition of Chinese archaeological objects, a very serviceable wash bucket, two very small and beautiful terracotta bowls, the star book.

2:10:90

Yesterday there was the book of indeterminate landscapes—Quebec. Today there was New Zealand and also, in various guises, Tonga. Gloria's kitchen was there too. Today I placed flowers—arriving fresh in their cellophane wrappers—in a large vase and filled the vase with water transported in a teapot. The teapot lives in a cardboard box near the kitchen department shelves—at the end nearest the fence.

Today I played with the sack of chromed letters at the new Revolve Yard. Outside the little shed with the brown door—where live the mannequins and their assorted clothes ... I made THEATRE—in big and little letters. There was no 'r' so I made it out of materials to hand—a squashed beer can, two glass tubes and a broken piece of wood.

(THEATRE stayed for some time, until at least the day that Cooleman court came in; huge and blue, twice. I made CALM and later, IMMORTAL ... Some days the letters fell down, but it was there for quite a while.)

I discovered that I could make ART with these letters and when I developed my writing shed, I placed these letters against it. I also found that if I turned the 't' upside down I could make AIR. These variations identified my spot in the yard for quite some time, but one day, like all things at the Tip, they simply disappeared.

Another way in which I worked with performance at the Tip was through following the transformations of one of Marilyn's sculptures made of found objects. This became *The Mermaid's Tale.*

I once read about an artist who started out writing short stories, then turned to concrete poetry, and finally became a gardener. This is a journey after my own heart.

20   KODAK 5053 TMY   21   KOD

making sense of the last ten years

melissa reeves

In 1985 I was working at Troupe Theatre in Adelaide as an actor. Most of the company had trained in acting at Flinders University with Julie Holledge and followed her to Troupe when she became the director. We worked there in a way that has very much shaped the way I look at theatre. The company was collective, it created a lot of new plays through commissioning writers to work through a conceptual, research and workshop process that involved everyone. It was concerned with being political, popular, and playing with the notion of theatre by altering the boundaries between the audience and performer, theatre that bent the rules and poached on popular forms, particularly in the series of dance narratives that had begun with *The Kelly Dance* (written with John Romeril).

The Red Shed Company that began a couple of years later, made up of another bunch of Flinders Drama Centre graduates, although a very different company with a very different feel, sort of groovier and with less overt political intentions, were also committed to making new work from the ground up as an ensemble company.

I wrote my first play *In Cahoots* for the Red Shed, and have worked consistently with them ever since. It's become increasingly apparent to me since beginning writing, the importance of operating in a group of people who know and respect each others' work, who share similar desires and enthusiasms, but who disagree enough with each other for the work to stay alive.

In 1988 I moved to Melbourne and was an unemployed actor and writing a play seemed a constructive way of filling time between the two paid jobs I got that year. I had two ideas for plays, one about landlords, a sort of revenge tragedy, and one about a Brownie meeting going mad. There being such an over abundance of female actors in the Shed—something like seven to one— Brownies seemed more practical so we went for that. The process was a bit ass-about, it being my first play. I wrote scenes and speeches before I'd worked out the story and got very attached to them, read them fondly and frequently and found myself in the position of having to inject a plot into a series of random scenes rather than build a series of scenes round a plot. It all started to hang together when I worked out the major twist to the story, that these Brownies would all be drastically over-age, and having discovered this feminist haven at an early age, had just stayed there ...

Commissioner	Don't play the innocent with me. You did exactly what I expected you to do. You couldn't tell a simple story of obedience and helpfulness without corrupting it. You think you're very clever don't you? At first I thought you were just bad Brownies, Brownies who drank and drove cars. You almost got away with it, but you forgot one vital thing. You're too big. (TO AUDIENCE) Do you really believe you are looking at girls of nine or ten, who all just happen to be too tall for their age? Two feet too tall. Well I'm not so stupid. This whole pack is riddled with over-age Brownies.
Natalie	I'm not too old am I?
Commissioner	How old are you?
Natalie	Sixteen.
Commissioner	You can't be a Brownie at sixteen.
Natalie	Well I'm only just sixteen.
Commissioner	What on Earth are you doing here?
Natalie	I don't know, I like ...
Commissioner	How old are the rest of you? Rhonda?
Rhonda	Seventeen.
Commissioner	Monica?
Monica	Nineteen.
Commissioner	Nineteen! That's disgusting. What would Lady Baden-Powell think of you?
Monica	She was a Guide at eighty-seven.
Commissioner	That's different. She was World Chief Guide.
Jeannie	Well why can't Monica be World Chief Brownie?

The play had a lot to do with my own experience of Brownies and how I felt I had inherited contradictory impulses from it—the "a Brownie is always cheery and a Brownie does her best" ethos as well as a sense of an anarchic adventurous army in leather belts and badges with secret societies and mad rituals. And then going on to Guides and having a rotten time with this sour, depressed sadist of a leader, it was sort of like the fun's over now, girls. To get more material I interviewed a lot of ex-Brownies and former Brown-Owls and Tawny-Owls and Guide Commissioners and really became addicted to this sort of first person research. I still find it one of the most exciting and nerve racking parts of writing plays.

I started interviewing the older women with a range of assumptions that were completely smashed. Walking into people's houses and asking all sorts of intimate questions and then racing off with the answers always feels strange for both parties, I think. At its best, it's fantastic to be taken so unawares, people's thoughts and stories and jokes and miseries can be so funny and bent, and often miles away from their stereotypical depiction—nuns when asked, so what does it mean to you, Mary Mackillop becoming a saint, saying I couldn't give a shit really. At its worst, it feels strangely sordid like I'm a thief, tricking people into divulging their secrets and pinching their best lines. Sometimes it feels important, recording, admittedly ultimately from my perspective, the perceptions of people who don't write about themselves, aren't written about, or are written about in a particular way. And always it feels privileged, taking me into people's private spaces that I would otherwise never enter, their loungerooms and kitchens, seeing their trinkets and trophies and choice of carpet.

To my chagrin to begin with, the play was particularly successful with Girl Guides and Guide Commissioners who turned up in droves, not realising what a hard hitting exposé of institutionalised disempowerment of women it was! And it made me realise you can be a lot harder than you think you can, that although the play said what I wanted it to, I had been pretty soft on everyone, even on the characters embodying the more poisonous aspects of the Guiding movement.

The experience of writing and putting on *In Cahoots* made me want to keep writing and although I kept performing, most of my acting jobs had an element of writing in them. Like Circus Oz where you often create your own work, and Short Arms Long Pockets in Melbourne with Margaret Mills and Maudie Davey, where we would improvise around ideas or aspects of ourselves—or in the second show, our mothers—for hours, and tape it all, then transcribe it and edit it and then perform this almost super-naturalistic, semi-autobiographical work. It's a very obsessive way of working. I found it very unsettling as well as absorbing but couldn't maintain that level of self-exploration and analysis for show after show. I think I prefer keeping myself apparently at one remove from the characters, even though I love watching and reading that sort of stuff.

For me, some of the pleasure of writing comes from control. I'm engaged in making a work that I can control absolutely. No-one can think anything without me thinking it first. Not only can I read everyone's mind, I am writing their minds, I am everyone, I am the masochist but also the hero, I am a child, I am an old woman, I am a man, I am a stupid man. I have so much control that I can let myself lose control, I am beyond time and beyond death, I am history, I am the future, I am god.

So at this stage it's a very privileged position. This megalomania all sounds very much at odds with what I was just saying about collaboration. But I think most aspects of working in the theatre have their own version of it. In reality, life sort of ambles along. I don't massively control it or make great overwhelming decisions, but in the play I make great swooping decisions. I really am some sort of god, sometimes letting these characters babble on from some untainted, murky place in my head, sometimes purposely pushing the characters into situations that will advertise what I think I want to say, getting malevolent pleasure from making them look idiotic, acting them out in my head and sometimes out loud, chuckling to myself at some really funny bit. Chucking sand about in some great big sand-pit. But always with the enormous freedom to cross it all out and start all over again.

In 1992 and 93 I wrote *Sweetown*. I started off wanting to write a play about a country town, having grown up in a country town, moving from the city with my mother; and I wanted to be quite vicious about it, because the town had been quite vicious, in a very morally underhand way. But after talking about ideas with the people that I talk about ideas with, I decided not to write directly about the town and the events I had experienced but to look for a more contemporary story and let my own story filter in where it wanted to. Around that time, there was a rash of country towns reputedly deciding to set up curfews to protect their youth. After ten o'clock all the teenagers had to be in bed which, if you went into it further, turned out to be more about putting the local young Aboriginal people under nightly house arrest. It seemed very rich material for a play but I hesitated because I didn't know how I could write about that sort of racism. There seemed so many pitfalls. What did I know about the experience of young Aboriginal kids? Was it my story to write anyway? But the fact that I *didn't* want to write about it worried me as well. Was I just avoiding the issue? Then I read *A Secret Country* by John Pilger and came across this story about a small country town in northern NSW that was near the site of a massacre that had occurred in 1838.

The Myall Creek Massacre was unusual in that the perpetrators—twelve men who worked on the stations in the area—were tried for the murder and seven of them were sentenced to death. Then in 1965, this bloke found some hinges near the site of the massacre and he believed them to be the hinges from the stockyard gate where the massacre happened. So he persuaded the local Apex Club to build a memorial gate as a reminder that this massacre occurred and to call for Aboriginal people to be granted citizenship and for attitudes to change. But the gate never got built. The proposal caused an uproar. The president of the local historical society wrote a vitriolic letter to the newspaper. The town became divided on the issue and the whole idea was dropped. So I decided to write the story of how in the first place, the local Apex Club, an institution with such a safe conservative sausage sizzle social position, got to the point of proposing what for the time was quite a progressive proposal, and then how the idea was destroyed by the historical society which was, of course, made up of land-owners of the district, who persuaded the town that the very idea of remembering this event was insulting to the history of Australia.

I decided to go to Bingara and interview people about the story. It was such recent history and all the people were probably still around. My mother had recently retired so she offered to drive me up there. She's a librarian so I generously made her my research assistant. By all accounts, the town was still very touchy about this whole episode and the closer we got to Bingara the more scared I got. The idea of rolling into this small town like Jana Wendt filled me with horror. It sounded much scarier than Tawny Owls, so by Tamworth I had decided that I wouldn't divulge my real intention, I would wander around incognito even though this seemed a draw-back if I actually wanted to interview anyone. Anyway, we arrived in town and put our stuff in the hotel and went down the pub for a drink and almost the first thing the publican says is, you know what Bingara is famous for and we said no and he said this was the first place white men were hung for killing blacks and I just sat there dumbfounded, but my research assistant who had a flair for this kind of thing said, "Really!" in a very loud, surprised and interested voice and the whole pub proceeded to elaborate on the history with a couple of guys at the end of the bar being casually and viciously racist.

The whole week took on a sort of clandestine feel. It was hard work convincing myself that I was allowed to write a play about this. I felt like I was committing some crime which must have been wrapped up in this notion of dirty secrets. And the town was very cagey and secret. I'd have people who had been in the Apex Club in 1965 saying after an hour or so of evasion, "Look, turn the tape off for a minute..." and I'd turn the tape off waiting for some big revelation. It also set me reading other accounts of massacres which I hadn't known about. Australia's history is so shocking. You start seeing history in such a different way, how blatantly genocidal the policies of the government and the land-owners were, how all the boys-own adventure and brave pioneer stories are hiding this bloody history and how you yourself have imbibed the falsehoods. This story seemed like a small breach in the armour of rigid happy official white history, a little chink that opened and caused shock-waves in the tiny community and then was expertly closed up again. It was an optimistic and a tragic story—optimistic in that people have the potential to change, but tragic in that the forces against change—media, historians, business and our own ingrained fears and bigotry—are incredibly powerful. This is a scene from early in the play where Miss Faversham, the local primary school teacher is teaching the history lesson ...

Miss Faversham   *I have marked last week's test and you can all have your papers back. Marjorie Werther, eight out of ten. Excellent. Rachel Greig, seven out of ten, also very good. Anthony Simmons, four out of ten, not very good. You can do better than that Anthony. I'd also like to point out to you that Francis Drake was never King of England and nor was Maid Marion.*

This week we begin a new chapter, the history of a country hundreds of miles away from England. A country I think you'll know something about already. During the sixteenth century many of the powerful countries of the northern hemisphere made expeditions in search of a great south land. Can anyone tell me who those countries were?

MARJORIE PUTS UP HER HAND.

Marjorie?

Marjorie   *America?*

Miss Faversham   *Very good. That's one. Anthony?*

Rachel   *Britain?*

Miss Faversham   *Write down in your books 'Pack your bags for down south'.*

SHE WRITES IT ON THE BLACKBOARD AND POINTS TO EACH WORD AS SHE IDENTIFIES THE COUNTRY.

P for Portuguese, B for Britain, F for French, D for Dutch, S for Spanish. The five powerful countries all in one handy sentence known as a mnemonic.

SHE WRITES THE WORD 'MNEMONIC' ON THE BOARD.

It's spelt very strangely isn't it? You'd think you'd say Mnemonic
wouldn't you? But you don't because the first M is silent.
We pretend the first M isn't there at all. Say it after me. Mnemonic.

All   *Mnemonic.*

Miss Faversham   *It's from the Greek word* mnemon: *to remember. Good.*
                            So did any of the five countries discover anything? Was there
                            a great south land?

NO-ONE PUTS UP A HAND.

                            A sun-burnt country? ... a land of sweeping plains ...
                            of rugged mountain ranges ...
                            ... of droughts and flooding rains

STILL NO HANDS.

                            The Commonwealth of ...

ALL PUT UP THEIR HANDS.

                            Yes alright.

All   *Australia.*

Miss Faversham   *Good. Write down in your books "Dairy cows save energy going*
                            slowly without tiring". Another handy mnemonic worth learning
                            by heart.

SHE WRITES THE SENTENCE UP ON THE BLACKBOARD.

                            The eight key points of Australian history. Discovery. Convicts.
                            Squatters. E ... Education. Gold. Ships. Sheep. Aaah ...
                            War, and of course the last one beginning with T which is of
                            course, Trains. Yes Marjorie?

Marjorie   *What about explorers Miss Faversham?*

Miss Faversham   *Well, yes they were very important.*
                            They can share the E with education ...

from *Sweetown*, 1994.

The other company that I've become involved with in writing as well as other capacities is Melbourne Workers' Theatre. MWT was formed about ten years ago by a group of theatre practitioners to make plays researched from the experience of working people and tour them round their work-places. It began with a very strong union base and received part of the Art-In-Working Life bracket of arts funding. Over the past few years of my involvement, the work-place as a site for performance has become less and less viable, the union support has dwindled as unions have come further and further under attack from the Victorian government and the company has had to constantly reassess what it wants to make theatre about, and who it wants to make it for. Also in what terms to describe itself. Meanwhile, there are constant battles being fought in Victoria involving large sections of communities protesting and positioning themselves against the government. There is also more and more a backlash against the left. The cry of political correctness is used as a weapon to make it appear that if somebody criticises anything, they are some boring, didactic goody-goody, and that notions like working-class, and socialism are relics from the past to be discarded along with the Berlin Wall and the Soviet Union. The whole idea was a big mistake. Any attempt to change the economic structure of society will lead to totalitarianism. Under capitalism you can have everything, choosing between the Labor version which pays lip service to things like feminism and land rights, or the Liberal version which just openly kicks most people in the teeth.

I think the role of the writer and the theatre is to expose the lies, reveal the secrets, illuminate the contradictions and all the while to celebrate the fantastic confusion of life. But I often get frustrated by how stupid I am when I'm writing. I constantly buy all these books—Noam Chomsky, Luce Irigaray— and mostly they sit in piles on my book-case, as though owning them is enough and I'm going to consume their contents by osmosis. I watch too much crap television and I've usually faded by the time I get to the world news in the newspaper. I've been struggling with writing a musical about Mary Mackillop for the Red Shed for nigh on three years. It's now up to its eighth draft and that has to be it because it goes on in November. The difficulty with it was it just seemed to be about everything. It's very irritating having piles of ideas, and endless books of notes, and fascinations about the multiplicity of forces in society and in people's heads and not to feel able to construct something that makes it all clear.

I got a shock recently when I read about some theatre person I admired saying the last thing they wanted to be was clear. I think the implication was that if something was clear it must be a bit of a lie, a reduction of something, because everything is such a confused amalgam of intention and history and power and desire. And I agree with that as well. I love the idea of uncomfortable, unfixed non-narrative work that isn't so analysed and sifted and sorted and balanced, that speaks on different levels, and I've enjoyed working in that way in collaboration with other people, but I also love the idea of big rambling epic narratives that make sense of the world, or make sense out of the senselessness. Like *One Hundred Years of Solitude* or *War and Peace* where all the events are played out remorselessly and inevitably or randomly and hilariously. So I don't want to get stuck in a particular style, or polarised into the narrative camp, to work at theatre as if there's a wrong and a right way to do it. I want to keep working with all possibilities in mind.

05:30 PM ─────────── interruption

PASSION

In the final session of the Festival, we held a preview screening of *Passion*, a three-part series featuring six plays by Australian women writers: *The Night of the Missing Bridegroom* by Linden Wilkinson, *The Gun in History* by Tobsha Learner, *Escape* by Jean Kittson, *Love Seen in Laundromat* by Lissa Benyon, *Flame* by Joanna Murray-Smith and *Barefoot* by Jennifer Compton. These works were initially produced by Ros Horin (Playworks founder) at the Griffin Theatre and produced for television by SBS Independent. The programs screened from December 17, 1995, Sunday nights at 8:30 pm. These plays are now published by Currency Press.

playing with time

MY   15   KODAK 5053 TMY   16

MY   15   KODAK 5053 TMY   16

the participants

Paula Abood wrote *The Politics of Belly Dancing* which explored images of importance to Arab-Australian women—issues of representation, cultural appropriation, cultural form and dance. It was staged at The Performance Space in Sydney and later at the Old Parliament House as part of the National Festival of Australian Theatre in Canberra. Paula, who describes it as a choreopoem, a dance text piece, also co-directed the production for Safa, an Arab women's community theatre group in NSW.

May-Brit Akerholt is the Artistic Director of the Australian National Playwrights Centre. She was Resident Dramaturg at the Sydney Theatre Company for six years and, before that, a lecturer in Drama and Dramaturgy at the National Institute of Dramatic Art (NIDA) and a tutor in English at Macquarie University. She has translated 12 plays for the Australian stage. She has published a book on Patrick White's plays and numerous articles in books and journals.

Andrea Aloise has devised and performed works with the Sydney Front, Entr'acte, Sidetrack Performance Group, One Extra Company and with Katia Molino. She is currently in a *where-do-I-fit in-with-this-theatre?* phase.

Virginia Baxter is the co-writer and co-producer of collaborative performance works for theatre, galleries and radio produced by Open City, the company she formed in 1987 with Keith Gallasch. Works include *The Girl With a Stone in her Shoe, All That Flows, Tokyo Two, The Museum of Accidents, Sense, Sum of the Sudden* and *Shop & The Necessary Orgy*. Virginia is currently working on *MondoLingo*, a CD Rom performance project on the subject of Australian Englishes. Virginia is co-editor of the national arts tabloid *RealTime* and the Chair of Playworks.

Katharine Brisbane is the Publisher of Currency Press, Australia's performing arts publishers. She was a theatre critic for 21 years. She has published widely on the history and nature of Australian theatre. She was a founder in 1972 of the Australian National Playwrights Conference and was Chair from 1985-90. Katharine Brisbane was a major contributor to the encyclopaedia *A Companion to Theatre in Australia,* published in September 1995.

Rosemary Cameron is a freelance arts administrator who has worked extensively in theatre, dance and film. She has provided project management for independent productions such as Alan Schacher's *Gravity Feed*, Chin Kham Yoke's *Inflamed*, The Independent Dance Collections 1994-95, Norman Hall's *Four Generations* and Sally Sussman's *Orientalia*. She has provided financial management for Griffin Theatre, Ausdance, Theatre of the Deaf, Shopfront, Dance Vision, Death Defying Theatre and Dance Base. Rosemary is the co-ordinator of the Sydney Arts Management Advisory Group.

Angela Chaplin has been Artistic Director of Deckchair Theatre for the last three years and previously of Magpie Theatre (State Theatre Company SA) where her productions included *White Paper Flowers* and *Couple of Kids* for the Come Out Festival and *The Arbor* for the Adelaide Festival. As Artistic Director of Melbourne's Arena Theatre (1985-88) she directed over 20 productions. As a member of the Mill Theatre Company in Geelong from 1981 to 1985 she worked as both actor and director and also took part in running the company's extensive community theatre program. Internationally, her productions have toured Canada and Japan and in 1992 she directed *Frankenstein's Children* for Teatro Nacional in Caracas, Venezuela. She was a member of the executive of ASSITEJ (The International Association of Theatre for Young People) from 1990 to 1993. For Deckchair, Angela directed and co-devised *Ningali* (which toured Edinburgh, Berlin and London) with Ningali Lawford and Robyn Archer.

Suzanne Chaundy was Dramaturg and then Associate Director of Anthill Theatre from 1981 to 1993. She has also worked for the Victoria State Opera, the West Australian Opera, the Melbourne Theatre Company, the Sydney Theatre Company, Griffin Theatre Co, Melbourne Writers' Theatre and La Mama. She has been a Victorian Representative for the Australian National Playwrights Centre since 1989 and teaches their courses in Melbourne, has been Artistic Director of the three Next Wave Young Playwrights Festivals and has worked as production dramaturg on over 20 plays. Recent work has included being Resident Director at the Third International Women Playwrights Conference, directing for the Victorian College of the Arts, for the Melbourne Symphony Orchestra, Australian Ballet, Victoria State Opera and Melbourne Theatre Company and working as Assistant Director to Ian Judge on his recent production of *Don Quixote* for the Victoria State Opera. Most recently Suzanne directed the world premiere of *Honey Baby: Thirteen Studies in Exile* by Deborah Levy for The Mission and La Mama.

Jennifer Compton's play *Crossfire* premiered at Nimrod Theatre and was published by Currency Press. It was joint winner with John Romeril's *A Floating World* of the Newcastle Playwriting Competition in 1974. Her one-act play *Julia's Song* premiered at Belvoir Street Theatre in 1993 and *Barefoot* (televised by SBS in 1995) was part of the *Passion* season at Griffin Theatre in 1994. *The Big Picture* (working title) her new play, was written with the aid of a Writers' Project Grant from the Australia Council and will be developed by Playworks in 1996. She has written many radio plays produced by ABC and RNZ. *The Goose's Bridle* won an AWGIE in 1976. Her first book of poetry *From the Other Woman* was published by Five Islands Press in 1993 and in 1995 she was awarded the NSW Writer's Fellowship to complete her second book, *Speaking with Voices*.

Cathy Craigie's produced work includes *Koori Love* (later re-named *Murri Love*) at Belvoir Street Theatre (Sydney) and for Kooemba Jdarra in Brisbane. She has also written a children's play *Murri Time,* which toured extensively throughout Queensland and at children's festivals in Adelaide and Sydney. A monologue, *Forever,* was written for the Sydney Festival in 1994 and produced by Theatre South.

Michelle Dado, designer and production manager for *Playing with Time,* graduated from the NIDA design course in 1988. She spent four years overseas based in the UK and the US where she worked in theatre, film and TV. In Los Angeles she art-directed a late night MTV style show called *Electric Coffee* and a documentary, *A Mother's Cry.* In London she designed ten theatre productions, including *The Ballad of the Limehouse Rat* which won a London Fringe Award for Best Production and London Festival Awards for Best New Play, Best Design, and Best Production. Since arriving back in Australia in 1994 she designed *Carthaginians* at Crossroads, *Europe* at Sydney's Stables Theatre, Playworks Showcase at the 3rd International Women Playwrights' Conference and *The Shoe-Horn Sonata* at the Ensemble Theatre. In 1994 she designed for Sydney's Seven Network and in 1995 *The Denton Show.*

Alma De Groen was born in New Zealand in 1941. In 1964 she settled in Australia where, under the influence of the new theatre movement, she began writing plays in 1968. While in Canada in 1970 she won a national playwriting competition with her short work, *The Joss Adams Show. The Sweatproof Boy* (later shortened *to Perfectly All Right*) was presented at the Nimrod Street Theatre in 1972. On her return to Australia *The Afterlife of Arthur Craven* was selected by the first Australian National Playwrights Conference (1973) and had a season the same year at Jane Street Theatre, Sydney. This was followed by *Going Home* (1976) and *Chidley* (1977) both of which had their premiere seasons in Melbourne. *Vocations* received a workshop at the 1981 Australian National Playwrights Conference and its premiere in Melbourne in 1982. Alma De Groen was awarded the 1985 AWGIE award for her television adaptation of *Man Of Letters* and has written scripts for the television series *Singles* and *Rafferty's Rules*. *The Rivers of China* was workshopped at the 1986 National Playwrights Conference and had its premiere in Sydney in 1987, winning the Premier's Literary Award for Drama in both NSW and Victoria. *The Girl Who Saw Everything* premiered at the Russell Street Theatre in Melbourne in 1991 and won the 1993 AWGIE for best stage play. Her most recent work is a radio play entitled *Stories In The Dark,* co-written with Ian D. Mackenzie, for ABC Radio's *Agenda Australia* series. She is currently working on a screenplay.

Anni Finsterer is a writer/performer. Recent writing credits include her one woman show *Gravegnomes,* performed as part of the Belvoir Street's *Open House* season. Anni has written and performed stand up comedy around Sydney and has also devised and performed a cabaret, *Desperately Seeking Moriah.* She has also collaborated on a pilot TV sitcom *Alive and Kicking.* She works as an actor in theatre, film and radio. Credits include: *The Loaded Ute* and the role of Cleopatra in *Antony and Cleopatra* for the Australian People's Theatre, touring *A Christmas Carol* to Asia and Europe with The American Drama Group, *Europe, The Wedding Song* for the NIDA Company and *The Threepenny Opera* for the Sydney Theatre Company.

Margaret Fischer is the Artistic Director of Vitalstatistix Theatre Company, based at Waterside, Port Adelaide, South Australia, a company which has been producing new works by Australian women playwrights since 1984. Margaret has been directing, collaborating, writing, performing and producing for twenty years. Originally from Sydney, she co-founded Pippi Storm—a ground-breaking company which toured Australia for a decade. For Vitalstatistix she has co-written many plays and produced 14 new works by Australian women playwrights. Her writing includes *The Gay Divorcee* and her new play *Wanted,* which she plans to tour to Adelaide, Sydney and New York. Also in progress is a play about divorce from a Jewish perspective for the Progressive Jewish Synagogue in Adelaide.

Venetia Gillot is a theatre director, dramaturg, cultural worker, writer and performer. Born in Durban South Africa, Venetia migrated to Australia in 1976. The focus of her theatre work over the past ten years has been the creation of new works for Australian audiences. Productions include: *The Last Drive-In on Earth* for Troupe, *What Do They*

Call Me by Eva Johnson, *Water from the Well* for Doppio Teatro, *Home Sweet Home* for Vitalstatistix (all in SA). In NT she has produced *Spilt Milk,* and *Muppulbah* for Corrugated Iron Youth Theatre, and *Keep Him My Heart—a Larrakia-Filipino Love Story* by Gary Lee. In 1994 she formed the women's cross cultural performance group Salt Fire Water. She is currently working with IAFAEK, Darwin's East Timorese cultural group on *Wall of Testimony* for a national tour later this year.

Jane Goodall is Associate Professor in the School of Humanities, University of Western Sydney, Hawkesbury campus, in a new interdisciplinary program which includes a degree in Postmodern Studies. Jane teaches courses in Cultural Change, Contemporary Arts, and "Postmodern Sydney". She has published widely on Australian performance and performance art and on avant-garde writing. Her book *Artaud and the Gnostic Drama—a study in ancient and modern heresies—*was published by Oxford University Press in 1994.

Clare Grant has been involved as actor/director in the creation of new works for theatre, radio and film for many years. She was a founding member of The Sydney Front, whose works over a period of seven years were staged at The Performance Space in Sydney and toured nationally and to Europe and Hong Kong. Clare has been associated with several other Sydney companies engaged in the devising of new works for theatre including Sidetrack Theatre, One Extra Company, Cake Eaters Productions, State Body Company and Entr'acte Theatre. In 1993 she collaborated with six other prominent Sydney women performers to create *Stages of Terror,* a work examining the theatricality of terror. Clare presented her solo performance *Woman in the Wall,* written in collaboration with Mickey Furuya, Nigel Kellaway and Sarah de Jong at The Performance Space in Sydney (1990) and at Artspace in Auckland, N.Z. (1992). With Virginia Baxter, she wrote and presented *Talking Back,* a performed conversation, at the Third International Women's Playwrights Conference in Adelaide (1994). Clare is currently Artistic Director of Playworks.

Dorothy Hewett, in addition to four screenplays, has written eighteen stage plays including rock operas (*Catspaw,* 1974 and *Pandora's Cross, 1978*), an opera (*Christina's World,*1983), three musical plays (*Bon-bons and Roses for Dolly,* 1972, *Joan,* 1975, *The Man from Mukinupin,* 1978), two children's plays, three radio plays and seven other major scripts, all of which include music, all of which have been published. Dorothy has received numerous senior writer's fellowships from the Literature Board of the Australia Council, has been writer-in-residence at many universities in Australia and overseas, was awarded the Order of Australia for her services to literature, and received a Keating Fellowship in 1992. She is Playworks' Patron.

Nikki Heywood is an experienced performer whose training includes Butoh. She has recently been engaged with the introduction of voice into physical performance in works such as *The Body Sings* (1993) and the major production of *Creatures Ourselves* (1995), both at The Performance Space.

Mary Hutchison began writing for performance professionally in 1980 when her first radio play was produced by the ABC. Since then she has written radio plays and documentaries, and her work, covering women's music/theatre, community theatre and visual/puppet theatre, has been produced by a variety of companies around Australia. She was introduced to puppet theatre by Spare Parts in WA, and has collaborated with the company on several productions, including the co-writing with Spare Parts' director, Peter Wilson, of *Overcoat.* Her most recent production was *Child of the Hurricane,* a performance inspired by the life and work of Katherine Susannah Prichard, with Women on a Shoestring, ACT. Over the last ten years Mary has worked as a writer in a variety of other forms—in particular the area of community writing and publishing. She has a strong interest in all forms of autobiography, in exploring different ways of using text in performance and in working collaboratively. Working on Skylark's (ACT) *Mum's the Word,* has offered her the opportunity to pursue all of these interests.

Sue Ingleton was a member of the APG Pram Factory Melbourne. Founding member of The Women's Theatre Group, Sue began writing and performing her own work at the forefront of political cabaret and stand up comedy, beginning with one woman shows *From Here to Maternity* and *Mothers Courage* in 1981. *Strip Jack Naked* was nominated for the Edinburgh Perrier Awards 1985 and selected for Montreal Juste Pour Rire 1986. *Near Ms's* (Adelaide Festival 1990 and Australian tour) won her the coveted Sidney Myer Individual Performing Arts Award 1989. She has written and directed for Circus Oz and artists Gerry Connolly and Sue Ann Post. She wrote the community play *Kindred Spirits* for Mallacoota Arts Festival and her most recent major work, *The Passion and its deep connection* with *Lemon Delicious pudding* was produced by Playbox at the Merlyn Theatre in 1995. Publications include *Sue Ingleton's Almanac,* and short stories in *Ink: The Follow Me Short Story Winners* and *The Marriage Tree* in *Weddings and Wives* edited by Dale Spender. Apart from her work as an actor and stand up comic, she teaches drama and creative writing and runs workshops in energy alignments and sacred theatre.

Noëlle Janaczewska writes for theatre, radio and print. Recent plays and scripts include: *Yungaburra Road, The Marie Curie Chat Show, Blood Orange, Fieldnotes,* and *The History of Water/Huyen Thoai Mot Giong Nuoc* which has been produced in Sydney, London and Canada and adapted for radio broadcast in Australia and Germany. Her new play *Cold Harvest* is being developed with Playworks.

Evdokia Katahanas is an actor who has done a lot of work with writer Tes Lyssiotis. Trained at the University of NSW and Victorian College of the Arts Evdokia has toured Indonesia with Entr'acte and performed with the Sydney Theatre Company, and at Belvoir Street Theatre, Theatre Royal, Stratford East. She has worked for many theatre companies including Toe Truck, Playbox and Theatreworks. On television she has appeared in *GP, Acropolis Now* and as Puck in *A Midsummer Night's Dream* for the ABC.

Jenny Kemp adapted and directed D. M. Thomas' *The White Hotel* in the early 1980s. In 1986 she wrote and directed *Good Night, Sweet Dreams* at Anthill Theatre in Melbourne. This was followed in 1989 with her *Call of the Wild* directed in collaboration with composer Elizabeth Drake, for the Melbourne International Festival with a season at Belvoir Street Theatre the following year. She collaborated with performer/writer Margaret Cameron or *Things Calypso Wanted to Say,* presented at Sydney's Performance Space in 1990. In 1991, she wrote and directed *Remember* (Gasworks, Melbourne). She has directed productions for the MTC and STCSA (including her ground-breaking production of Botho-Stauss *Big and Little* in 1985). Her new work *The Black Sequin Dress* has been commissioned for the 1996 Adelaide Festival. Jenny teaches at the VCA and Victorian University.

Ningali Josie Lawford has just completed a very successful overseas tour of *Ningali,* in which she uses three languages, storytelling, traditional song, country and western music to tell her unique story: from her birth at Christmas Creek Station in WA's far north, the adventures of her rodeo riding brothers, Walmajarri traditions, to living as an exchange student in Alaska. She is soon to tour again for the Kimberley Aboriginal Medical Service in a production of *No Prejudice,* a play about AIDS that Ningali is involved in as actor and script consultant. In December she travels to Alaska to present a radio program in a series titled *The Off Season.* She has several film offers pending and a invitation to the NZ Festival in 1996. She has performed for Deckchair Theatre Company, Eureka Productions, the ABC in *Heartlands* and with Black Swan Theatre Co in *Bran Nue Dae.*

Tobsha Learner writes for theatre, film, radio and television. Her plays have been produced by theatre companies throughout Australia. Among her many successful works are: *Witchplay, S.N.A.G., Miracle, Wolf, Mistress, The Glass Mermaid*. Her radio plays include *Volkov* and *Lionheart* (winner of the Silver Medal at the 1993 New York International Radio Competition). In 1995 she directed her latest play *Seven Acts of Love (as witnessed by a cat)* at Budinski's Theatre of Exile in Melbourne. Her short play, *The Gun in History* was featured in the SBS *Passion* series.

Jacquie Lo May Lye dances between the hyphenated spaces of a Chinese-Malaysian-Australian identity. She is presently a lecturer in drama at the University of Newcastle.

Alison Lyssa's new play *Where There's A Will* is featured in this year's Playworks program. Her other plays include *The Boiling Frog,* Nimrod 1984, published by Currency/Nimrod 1984; *Pinball,* Nimrod 1981, published in *Plays by Women Vol IV,* ed M. Wandor, Methuen, London NY 1985; *Who'd've Thought?* a community play written with the Women's Theatre Project, Telopea Theatre Group 1990, nominated for an AWGIE 1991; and a screenplay, *The Silk,* adaptation of a story by Joy Crowley, AFTRS 1993, 17 mins, AFI nomination for Best Screenplay in a Short Film 1994, ATOM Award 1995.

Tes Lyssiotis has been working in theatre since 1979. She has written and directed several productions for La Mama in Melbourne including *I'll Go to Australia and Wear a Hat; Come to Australia, They Said* and *On the Line*. She wrote and directed the multi-lingual play *Hotel Bonegilla* at La Mama, the Universal Theatre, Melbourne and then toured it. In 1985 Tes wrote and directed a trilogy entitled *The Journey* at La Mama. It subsequently played at the Universal Theatre and the Antipodes Festival, and toured Victoria, NSW and Queensland. Her play *A White Sports Coat* played at La Mama and Theatreworks, Melbourne and toured extensively. In 1990 Tes was commissioned by Playbox Theatre to write a bi-lingual play, *The Forty Lounge Cafe* (published by Currency Press). Her *Blood Moon* (1993) was performed at Theatreworks, Melbourne and Theatre West, Perth.

Sarah Miller is currently Director of the Perth Institute of Contemporary Arts (PICA) whose programs encompass a complex mixture of exhibition, performance, work-shop, forum, artist-in-residency and cultural exchange projects. Prior to this she was Director of The Performance Space, Sydney. Her own practice—now sadly intermittent—encompasses performance-making and critical writing. Throughout the 80s she worked with the performance group *Told by an Idiot* (with Adrienne Gaha and Derek Kreckler) devising and performing works throughout Australia and the UK. Her most recent collaborative project was *Stages of Terror,* an all women performance project which premiered at The Performance Space during 1993. She has written and spoken extensively on cultural policy at both state and national levels. She would rather write thrillers.

Caitlin Newton-Broad is Assistant Administrator for the Festival and Administrator for Playworks. She has a B.A Communications (UTS) and is currently undertaking a part-time MA in performance, installation and film at College of Fine Arts UNSW. Caitlin writes and makes object-performances. She is also a dedicated spectator.

Pamela Payne is the Theatre Critic for the *Sun Herald* in Sydney, an arts writer and commentator. She was Director of Playworks in 1993. Her essay *Reviewing Theatre in Draughty Halls* appeared in the Spring 1994 edition of *Meanjin.*

Deborah Pollard's solo works include *Eat Cake* and *Mother Tongue Interference.* She has created a number of works in collaboration with Victoria Spence, most notably *The Fall of the Roman Empire* and *Dripping with Ennui.* Deborah has worked with companies Entr'acte, Cake Eaters and Jigsaw Theatre and has worked on performance installation projects in Indonesia. She is currently working on a new performance, *Fish Out of Water.*

Melissa Reeves is a writer and sometime performer. Her plays include *In Cahoots* and *Sweetown* for Adelaide's Red Shed Company, *Great Day* for Melbourne Workers' Theatre and *The Song of the Phantom* for Theatre of the Deaf. Her musical comedy *Storming Heaven* for Red Shed premiered in 1995 at the Adelaide Festival Centre.

Sally Richardson is a writer-director and performer. Her produced works include *Picasso and Francoise* (1991), *Hang-Ups* (1991), *Ready or Not* (1992), *Kamarade* (1992), *So is it a Lover?* (1992), *Five Fingers* (1993) *Death in the House* (1994). She has produced works with ABC Radio, WA Academy of Performing Arts, Skylark Theatre, Tango 160, O'Punsky's Theatre, ANPC, SWY Theatre, New Stages (STC), N.I.D.A. and University of WA. While co-director of Playworks she directed Playworks' 1994 program for the Third International

Women's Playwrights' Conference. She is currently co-ordinator of Stages (W.A. Playwrights Consortium) and her new work *I Am Nijinsky* is scheduled for production in 1995. A published writer, journalist and poet, Sally has also worked as radio producer, dramaturg and assessor.

Victoria Spence has worked in performance as an image maker, writer, conceiver, teacher, collaborator, stage manager, technician, performer and audience member. She has worked in theatres, galleries and site-specifically. She has created a number of short solo pieces, worked in collaboration with Deborah Pollard, is a founding member of Women Theatre Company and has worked in various capacities with Peggy Wallach, Derek Kreckler, The Sydney Front, Sidetrack Performance Group, Cake Eaters Productions, Splinters Theatre of Spectacle, and Post Arrivalists. Solo work includes *For Medicinal Purposes Only, Vicki's B'day Party;* Eventspace, The Performance Space, *Waiting* for *25 years of Performance Art in Australia.* Work created with Deborah Pollard includes *The Fall of the Roman Empire* at the Ralph Wilson Theatre, Gorman House and *Dripping With Ennui,* Gyles Gym, Coogee.

Suzanne Spunner is a playwright, designer and dramaturg. She was a founding member of Home Cooking Theatre Company in Melbourne and wrote *Not Still Lives, Running up a Dress, The Accompanist, Edna for the Garden* and *Safe 'n' Sound.* In 1987 she moved to Darwin and formed Paradise Productions and wrote/designed *Dragged Screaming to Paradise, Overcome by Chlorine, Radio for Help* and *The Inkata's Wife.* Suzanne also writes for film and radio.

Amanda Stewart is a poet interested in language and its relationship to the voice. Since the late 1970s she's been involved in a range of performances, radiophonic works and film and video projects in Australia, Japan, the US and Europe. Lately, she's been exploring 'oral grammars' and disjunctions between aural and graphic forms of inscription (ie 'modes of memory'). Recent work available includes ‡ (Leonardo CD Series 3, MIT Press, USA, 1993), *on second thoughts* CD with Australian group, Machine for Making Sense (00 Discs, USA, 1994) and *Eclipse of the Man-Made Sun*, a 55 mm film made with Nicolette Freeman (film or video, Ronin Films, Australia, 1992).

Peta Tait is the author of *Converging Realities: Feminism in Australian Theatre* (1994) and *Original Women's Theatre* (1993). Her plays include *Deadlock* (1988), *Mesmerised*

(1992) co-written with Matra Robertson, and *Appearing in Pieces,* a group project produced with The Partyline in 1993 at The Performance Space.

Katherine Thomson is a playwright and actor who began her career in 1969 with the Australian Theatre for Young People. She was a founding member of Theatre South in Wollongong, where her first play, *A Change in the Weather* was produced in 1982. In 1984 the company produced and toured her next play, *Tonight We Anchor in Twofold Bay,* which also had a season at the Wharf Studio. Katherine's *A Sporting Chance* (1987) was produced in most states of Australia by theatre-in-education companies, and in 1988 *Darlinghurst Nights* was produced by the Sydney Theatre Company and adapted for ABC Radio National. Her 1991 production *Diving for Pearls* (Currency Press) has had seasons all over Australia and was awarded the Victorian Premier's Literary Award. Also in 1991 she wrote *Barmaids* (Currency Press) for Deckchair Theatre, which was also performed at Belvoir Street Theatre, State Theatre Company of South Australia, New England/Theatre South and Fortune Theatre in New Zealand and won an Australian Writers' Guild Award in 1992.

Alana Valentine is the recipient of a NSW State Literary Award, a Churchill Fellowship and the 1994 ANPC New Dramatists Award. She has written and directed a short flim *Mother Love,* written several stage plays including *Shudder* and *Southern Belle* and three radio plays *The Story of Anger Lee Bredenza, Screamers* and *Oysters at the Paragon.* Alana has recently written a film for the new Museum of Sydney, called *The Witnesses,* which is installed on laser disc in the museum. Her play *The Conjurers* was read at this year's Australian National Playwrights Conference. She is currently under commission to the Freewheels Theatre Company in Newcastle.

Margaret Williams is a senior lecturer in Theatre and Film Studies at the University of NSW, where she has been teaching for the last 23 years. Subject areas include courses on Women and Theatre at both undergraduate and postgraduate levels. Before that she was a tutor at Monash University while completing her PhD (on nineteenth century Australian Theatre) and a member of the Australian Performing Group at the Pram Factory in the early 70's. Among Margaret's publications is a monograph on Dorothy Hewett (Currency Press).

thank you

acknowledgements

PLAYWORKS ACKNOWLEDGES SUPPORT FROM:

FILM AND THEATRE STUDIES, THE UNIVERSITY OF NEW SOUTH WALES

COLLEGE OF FINE ARTS, THE UNIVERSITY OF NEW SOUTH WALES

CENTRE FOR PERFORMANCE STUDIES, SYDNEY UNIVERSITY

THE SYDNEY THEATRE COMPANY

VICTORIAN WRITERS CENTRE

UNIVERSITY OF NEWCASTLE

PACT YOUTH THEATRE

La Boite Theatre

During the past twenty-five years La Boite has been forging an enviable local and national reputation for producing sharp, contemporary Australian Theatre. The company is well known for encouraging new and local talent, and fostering original work by local playwrights. In 1999 La Boite is presenting four new works by Queensland playwrights including Jill Shearer's award winning *Georgia* and the return of Margery Forde's highly successful *X-Stacy*.

Women playwrights who have had their work produced by La Boite Theatre include Hilary Beaton, Sara Hardy, Karin Mainwaring, Alana Valentine, Peta Murray, Sue Rider, Maryanne Lynch, Helen Howard, Elizabeth Jolley, Sue Woolfe, Hilary Bell and Jennie Swain.

La Boite is currently accepting scripts for consideration for future production and development initiatives. Playwrights interested in submitting their work should forward a clearly typed copy of the script, together with a stamped-self-addresses envelope to:

The Play Advisory Committee
La Boite Theatre
57 Hale Street
Brisbane, Queensland 4000

School of Contemporary Arts
UWS Nepean

dance **theatre** **music** **fine arts**

<u>Undergraduate & Post - Graduate Degrees</u>

Key areas of research opportunities include collaborative and hybrid practice, multimedia and new technologies, theatre, musicology, dance, contemporary performance, Asian and Aboriginal cultures, gender and space, visual communication, site-specific work, professional practice.

for more information please contact:

Dance Wendy Pritchard
Tel: (02) 4736 0208
Fax: (02) 4736 0166
Email: w.pritchard@nepean.uws.edu.au

Music Ivanka Banach
Tel: (02) 9685 9766
Fax: (02) 9698 976
Email:i.banach@nepean.uws.edu.au

Theatre Sue Sheehy
Tel: (02) 4736 0646
Fax: (02) 4736 0241
Email: s.shehhy@nepean.uws.edu.au

Fine Arts Sandra Wantuch
Tel: (02) 4736 0468
Fax: (02) 4736 0204
Email: s.wantuch@nepean.uws.edu.au

home page: http://www.nepean.uws.edu.au/arts/